The Healthcare Manifesto

The Ultimate Handbook for Owners, CFOs, CEOs, and anyone who has to manage the COST of benefits

Copyright © 2021

All rights reserved. No part of this publication may be reproduced, distributed, or transmitted in any form or by any means, including photocopying, recording, or other electronic or mechanical methods, without the prior written permission of the publisher, except in the case of brief quotations embodied in critical reviews and certain other noncommercial uses permitted by copyright law.

ISBN: 978-1-7373243-0-0

Disclaimer

Any U.S. tax advice contained herein was not intended or written to be used, and cannot be used, for the purpose of avoiding penalties that may be imposed under the Internal Revenue Code or applicable state or local tax law provisions.

This information is for educational purposes only and is not intended, and should not be relied upon, as tax or legal advice. Recipients of this document should seek advice based on their particular circumstances from an independent tax advisor or legal counsel.

Everything is subject to change depending upon the whims of the Federal Government and the Rules written.

Table of Contents

Foreword..1

My Healthcare Manifesto......................................3
    We Don't Have to Continue..4
    Say No To Unsustainable Rate Increases.............................5
    Who Does This New Program Work For?................................6
    Why Me? From Health Insurance Broker to a Benefits Consultant......7
    Enter LinkedIn...8
    Understanding How to Rebuild a Watch..............................10
    Ascend – The Second Year..11
    Today...11

Introduction and Overview................................. 13
    How Much Would Health Insurance Cost If You Had No Claims?.......13
    A Good Year Still Results in a Rate Increase.....................15
    Opening the Hood on a Health Insurance Policy....................16
    How Do Insurance Companies Design Health Plans?..................18
    Fully Insured Health Plans.......................................21
    ASO Contracts..22
    Level-Funded Health Plans..23
    Self-Insured Health Plans..23
    It's Not an All or Nothing Method................................24
    The Rest of the Book...25

Chapter 1
4 Kinds of Risk Management................................ 29
    Four Ways to Manage Risk...30
    Takeaway Tips..32

Chapter 2
Managing Pharmacy Costs................................... 35
    What You See Is Not What You Get.................................37
    You Can Do Something About Pharmacy Costs........................40
    Takeaway Tips..44

Chapter 3
Managing Hospital Costs 47

It's the Frequency and Severity of Claims 48
How To Reduce the Frequency of Claims: Data First 48
Manage Chronic Conditions 50
Require Second Opinions 51
Require Levels of Treatment 53
Move Procedures to Outpatient Surgery 54
Use a Medical Management Company 55
Takeaway Tips 55

Chapter 4
Managing Outpatient Surgery Costs 57

If You Can't Avoid Outpatient Surgery 58
Websites to Review Doctors and Hospitals 62
Takeaway Tips 64

Chapter 5
Managing Physician Visits 67

Direct Contracting 68
Set Up a Clinic 69
Ask for A Rate Reduction from the TPA 70
Telemedicine 70
EAP and Mental Health 72
Takeaway Tips 73

Chapter 6
How Taking on Risk can Reduce Cost 75

Fully Insured Plans 76
Fully Insured with an HRA/MERP 76
Level-Funded/Partially Self-Funded Plan 78
Coalition 80
Self-Funded 81
Direct Contracting and/or Reference-Based Pricing 81
Takeaway Tips 83

Chapter 7
The Importance of Second Opinions and Medical
Management 85

Takeaway Tips 88

Chapter 8
Be Your Own Advocate 89
   Takeaway Tips 91

Book Summary 93
   Consolidated Listing of All Tips 94
   10 Bonus Tips..98

Bonus Material.. 101
   Epilogue - Managing the Rapid Pace of Change....................101
   What Do I Do Next?...108

Before You Go... 109

Thank You to Our Reviewers............................ 111

Appendix.. 115
   Insurance Terminology 115

Endnotes 121

ROBERT C SLAYTON, MS Ed - BIOGRAPHY 125

Foreword

Healthcare shouldn't be hard. It should serve as a way for everyone to get the care they need when they get sick. However, the system is convoluted, cumbersome, and can frustrate even the most patient of people. The United States continues to spend more on healthcare than any other developed nation, yet our standard of care keeps going down. The cost of healthcare has gone up every single year since 1960, and it doesn't seem like that trend will change any time soon.

There's no question the system is broken—but how do we go about fixing it?

Part of the solution is helping uncover healthcare's biggest lie: that employers don't have any control over the cost of healthcare. We do! Robert Slayton's book provides tangible ways to help the reader understand what's really happening in their health insurance contract.

As employers, learning how to navigate one of the top 3 most costly expenditures in business is invaluable. As beneficiaries of healthcare, the more we know about the current system, the less frustrating it can become. This book provides practical ideas on the current cost drivers, reducing those costs, and specific tactics we can use as employers to provide higher quality care at a lower cost.

Before you read this book, take stock of where you're at with your healthcare expenses. Where do you want to see them, how much are you currently paying, and how much do you want to pay? Then, read the book and apply what you learned to your own assessment. It's time that we take the time to learn how to better manage our healthcare costs. If you're saying, 'you don't have time,' you better make time. It'll save you a lot of money in the long run that you can use to grow your business, and make you a savvier consumer. Find the time, read the book, reap the benefits.

> Jeffrey Hayzlett ~ Primetime TV & Podcast Host, Chairman & CEO C-Suite Network, Keynote Speaker, Best-Selling Author, and Global Business Celebrity

My Healthcare Manifesto

Strong Words from a formerly frustrated Broker

The time has come to wake up and realize that giving a person a health insurance card and thinking that is enough is a thing of the past.

The time has come to wake up and realize that as an employer, you do not have to suffer the pain of unsustainable renewals of your health insurance plan.

Offering health insurance is not enough anymore. Employers need to do more. Assuming an insurance company will take care of your employees is a fiction that can no longer be tolerated. Ceding power to both the insurance company and healthcare providers leads to higher costs, higher premiums, and poorer outcomes.

> We as employers need to <u>do</u> more
>
> We as employers need to <u>be</u> more

Employers need to take a more proactive approach, one where we say "Enough is enough." Or as the character, Howard Beale in the classic movie *Network* stated, "I'm Mad as Hell, and I'm Not Going to Take It Anymore" [1].

We don't have to submit to zero control over health insurance premiums. We don't have to submit to poor care, expensive medications that may not work, nor to no transparency.

Why do we, as patients, use the "hope-and-pray" model of care? We Hope that our doctor made the correct diagnosis. We Pray that we are given the best doctors/specialists/surgeons. We Pray that the treatment works.

We Don't Have to Continue

Right Now, we can gain control over costs for both premiums AND healthcare.

Right Now, we can gain control over our quality of care – thereby driving better outcomes. Right Now, people are waiting to help and guide us as patients through the complicated health care maze of diagnosis and treatment.

Data is available today such that we can confirm we have the right diagnosis, which leads to the right treatment by the right doctor at the right facility, for the right price.

What happens when we do this? Costs go down!

We can be a hero to employees because instead of raising employees' premiums, we lower it.

We can also be a hero to employees because instead of raising employees' deductible and out-of-pocket maximum, we lower it.

We can even help an employee get the expensive surgery they need at no cost to the employee and still save money for the employer.

Say No To Unsustainable Rate Increases

We can be a hero to the bottom line and board of directors because we can take control of the health care and health insurance spend. Once that's achieved, we'd be the only people who can control an "uncontrollable" expense.

Gone are the days when your insurance agent gives you a 10% or 20% rate increase, then "negotiates" it down to 8%, saying that this increase is "below trend." These are fictions caused by ceding control to a person who makes more money the higher your premiums climb and insurance companies who design plans and pricing to make a profit.

Who Does This New Program Work For?

This does not work for employers who do not contribute to the cost of their employees' insurance.

This does not work for employers who contribute a flat dollar amount towards their employees' insurance.

The reason is that there are no-cost savings to the employer, which can be shared between the employer and employees.

This plan does work for companies that contribute a significant portion to the cost of coverage (at least 50%). Our philosophy is that both the employer and employee share in the benefits of the new order.

This plan does work for companies willing to champion the new model as it gets implemented (typically over 3 – 5 years).

People are dying because of the old Hope and Pray model. It doesn't have to be this way.

If you've had enough of the Hope and Pray model of Hoping your annual health insurance renewal won't be "too bad" and if you're fed up with Hoping that employees are diagnosed correctly and Praying they have the right treatment plan, then join me.

Join me in the NEXT GENERATION Revolution.

- Better care
- Better outcomes
- Lower cost

Let's break the cycle of mediocrity together.

Find out how by emailing me at breakthecycle@robert-slayton.com.

Why Me? From Health Insurance Broker to a Benefits Consultant

I was frustrated. The Affordable Care Act (ACA) had upended the apple cart. Commissions were flat. The premiums were spiraling out of control and although I was actually making more money than before the ACA, it was frustrating.

After spending numerous hours reading the Act, seeking expert opinions, and helping clients navigate this new act, the employer and employee costs still went up, up, up. Furthermore, the deductibles and out of pocket maximums kept increasing to manage the costs.

Then the customer service we needed to do for clients doubled, tripled, and quadrupled due to both extra requirements and insurance carriers shedding senior representatives in order to save cost. What the insurance companies used to do for clients, they no longer did with the effectiveness of pre-ACA. The networks were narrowing and doctors were opting out in the middle of the year leaving some of the employers' members without a doctor or specialist they trusted.

I was stuck. Nothing was helping either the employers or employees. It was just more seeking quotes from multiple insurance companies, putting them on a spreadsheet, and helping the employer pick the "least bad" plan that they could afford.

It wasn't fun anymore. My value was limited to ACA consulting and the usual day-to-day tasks.

I started looking for solutions. Studying self-funded plans, captives, large groups, and what was going on in the industry, both from a health insurance perspective and health care provider. I wanted to find some happy medium where both I and the employer had more control over both the insurance system and the health care world.

Enter LinkedIn

I've been on LinkedIn since its inception and make it a habit of connecting with new and interesting people. One of those people was Gary Becker of ScriptSource. When reading his bio, he seemed to be doing the things I wanted to do. So I messaged him asking whether we could hop on a call so I could pick his brain.

Gary replied that if I really wanted to understand this world, there was an event coming up in a couple of weeks in Nashville called *Ascend*. When I got around to looking (the night before), it seemed to fit the bill. People were talking about ways to reduce the cost of insurance through new and innovative methods. Furthermore, the vendors were all vetted by other members so if I wanted to use them, I knew they did what they promised.

The only problem was that the conference started the very next day , so I messaged Nelson Griswold (one of the two founders) at 9 pm, asking whether there was still space. He responded at 2 am that *yes*, there was and I was welcome to come. So at 5 am I booked a hotel room, hopped in my car, and drove to Nashville, arriving about 2 hours after the start.

It was eye-opening. It was drinking from a fire hose. Other agents were happy, successful, giving of their time and knowledge. Vendors understood the issues facing employers and had developed solutions to help them reduce the cost of their insurance spend but also increase the quality of care for employees.

Loaded down with vendor materials, business cards of agents who said I could call them anytime, and more energy for this business than I'd had in years, I drove home and proceeded to spend the next two months calling every vendor to get a one-on-one for what they do, what size and profile businesses they work with, how I enter the relationship (e.g. how to present their solution), how to onboard, and how (if) I was compensated for bringing their solution.

I spent the next year educating myself on what was going on in the healthcare industry and health insurance industry so that I knew which solutions solved which problems and how they played with other solutions and the impacts it had on both management and employees at an employer.

Understanding How to Rebuild a Watch

I liken this process to becoming a tinker of health insurance/health care. A tinker repairs and can even build a mechanical watch. They have to first understand the parts of the watch and what each does before they can pull a piece out and replace it with another.

Sometimes it's just replacing something like a sprocket, other times it is taking all the components out of the watch and rebuilding it such that it will work much better than before. If you've ever tried to replace a spring in a watch or anywhere else, if done incorrectly, the spring and all its components explode all over the floor.

Diagnosing and rebuilding an employee benefit plan is similar in that there are a lot of moving parts. If done correctly, it works like a train engineer's watch. If done incorrectly, it will cause a lot of headaches that someone has to constantly manage.

Ascend – The Second Year

Attending Ascend for the second year, I was finally able to put the pieces together in my brain. No fish-eyed overwhelm the first year. From that point, I joined NextGen Mastermind Partners, a group of 50 benefit advisers who are on the cutting/bleeding edge of benefit plan design and implementation.

Through this network of highly skilled advisers, solutions are found and implemented for clients. I was starting to have fun again and hanging out with people who had the same beliefs as I did about sharing knowledge, the industry, and how to most effectively respond.

Today

I've redesigned my business such that there are two categories. The first are the traditional clients, those we can't do as much with because of their size, contribution strategy, lack of desire, or other characteristics. The second are those NextGen clients who buy into creating something new, bold, beautiful, and helpful to themselves and their employees.

I have a team of dedicated employees to help with the traditional clients because they still need help and we can help them. The NextGen clients are served by me and my staff that help with the administration of the strategies we've put into place. It is not so much day-to-day things, but managing the overall program, quality, and profitability.

We can either charge a fee or are willing to work on a performance guaranteed basis. If what we do doesn't save you money, then you don't have to pay us. If it does (and it does), then you pay us 1/3 of the savings. This way we are sitting on the same side of the table as you, the employer. We only make money when you save money—when your costs go down. That's the best deal out there.

Introduction and Overview

As you can see from my "manifesto" I'm upset with how bad things have become in both the healthcare and health insurance arenas. The good news is that we can do something about it. The purpose of this book is to help you understand the risk, cost, and quality drivers so that you can help take control of the second-largest line item in your budget.

How Much Would Health Insurance Cost If You Had No Claims?

You read that right. If you had health insurance and incurred no claims, how much "should" it cost? It's a trick question because within health insurance is "insurance" against major claims and then administration, pharmacy, network, wellness, and other expenses. The larger the company, the smaller the "insurance" cost is.

When you hear the word "health insurance renewal," most think it means the total cost of the plan you are on. For example, let's say that your health insurance renewal went up 10%, so your total monthly cost for the insurance went up 10%. The reality is that only a portion of that plan is covered by insurance. For large, self-insured companies, the insurance portion of the cost may be just 5%. So a 10% increase on the insurance portion adds .5% to the total plan cost.

Another concept to understand is that if you are on a fully insured plan, then you are pre-paying for claims that haven't occurred yet and may never happen. If you don't use the plan, then that extra money goes into the health insurance company's profit.

Health insurance companies estimate the number and cost of claims for the year, and then add a little bit to this just in case they underestimated it. If you have a healthy group who rarely go to the doctor, then all of those potential claims never come to pass, but you've already paid for them through your premium.

A final concept is that most insurance agents are compensated as a percentage of the premium you pay. This means that when your insurance cost goes up, your agent makes more money. Furthermore, most get paid a "retention" bonus for staying with one carrier.

What this means is that incentives are misaligned. Your agent wants your insurance cost to go up because they make more money. They also want you to stay with your existing fully insured insurance company because they make a lot of money (which they *do not* have to report on a Form 5500) when you do.

So, if you ever wonder why the same carrier "always" seems to be the best deal, it may be because your agent is cooking competitive quotes. Oh, and if you switch insurance companies? Sometimes, insurance companies pay bonuses to agents for placing business with them, and those bonuses are larger than the retention bonus with the existing insurance company.

A Good Year Still Results in a Rate Increase

Isn't it amazing that your health insurance premiums still go up even if you have a great year?

Remember this: for all but the smallest employers (on ACA-mandated small group health insurance), your insurance's cost is based on the frequency and severity of claims. If you can put in place tools and controls to minimize the frequency of claims (how many) and severity of claims (cost), then your health insurance costs will be less (premium to the employer and employees).

We've been able to cut costs for our employer clients by up to 40% while providing *better* outcomes for employees, resulting in lower costs for both employees and employers.

Opening the Hood on a Health Insurance Policy

Unless you are one of the few who truly understands the world of insurance, your health insurance plan is treated more or less like a black box: impenetrable. The reality is that ALL health insurance plans include the same components.

First is a sales and service team. This includes your broker and the marketing and sales department at the insurance company, a program manager for implementing a plan, etc. Second is a way to administer the plan, commonly known as a "Third Party Administrator."

Shockingly, many of the biggest names in the health insurance business farm part of all of it out to other companies such as Meritain and UMR. These people check the member's eligibility and claims, process the standard claims, make sure network discounts are applied, and all of the day-to-day items that touch the member.

The third is the network (if used). Some have their own networks, such as Blue Cross Blue Shield, and some rent networks such as Multiplan, First Health, and many others. If a company is not using a network, then there would be a component for managing the cost of the claims if the provider rejects payment.

Fourth deals with prescriptions. These companies are known as "Pharmacy Benefit Managers" (PBM). They are the middle people between the insurance company (or employer) and drug manufacturers. Their goal is to have purchasing agreements that make sure that you get the drugs at a discount. This is by far the most profitable segment for the health insurance plan and why most of the big players have either purchased or been purchased by a health insurance company.

Fifth is "Medical Management" for people with major conditions such as cancer, rare and expensive diseases, chronic conditions that cost a lot to manage, etc. The big players almost always farm this out in the marketplace. This is also the place where you can positively impact your employees if you choose the right company.

Finally, you have reinsurance. Suppose a claim costs too much money. In that case, the insurance company doesn't want to be on the hook for millions of extra dollars. Companies use a reinsurance company such as Swiss Re to reinsure major claims or over a cap of multiple claims (aggregating all claims together and if it exceeds a certain amount, then the reinsurance company pays everything above that). Reinsurance reduces the risk of an awful year. Here's a graphic of how it may look:

Components of A Fully-Insured Health Plan

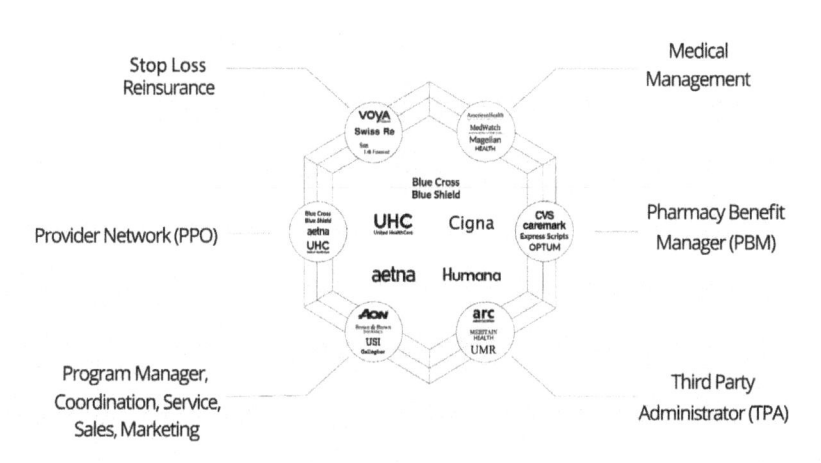

- Stop Loss Reinsurance
- Medical Management
- Provider Network (PPO)
- Pharmacy Benefit Manager (PBM)
- Program Manager, Coordination, Service, Sales, Marketing
- Third Party Administrator (TPA)

Graphic Courtesy of Nelson Griswold

The interesting part about this graphic is that the insurance company puts itself in the middle. They are the focus. When we design plans, we put BOTH the employer and member in the middle because that's the way it should be.

When a company uses an alternative funding mechanism (explained below), they use THE EXACT SAME COMPONENTS. The difference is you can choose the components and switch them out at any time. Instead of using a PBM that refuses to be a fiduciary for your plan (as most big players do), you can choose a PBM that charges a flat fee and ALL money and rebates flow back to the employer.

This is especially important with specialty drugs. If you are a large employer and have been told you get the rebates back, check your contract. There is a real possibility that they only give the rebates back on standard drugs, but they keep the rebates on specialty drugs (where the money is). Check it out. You'll be shocked when you do.

How Do Insurance Companies Design Health Plans?

The simple answer to the question is "to make a profit." Insurance companies design plans to make a profit, NOT to make sure you get the best care. Each company has to meet the state or federal mandates (for example, in Illinois, fully insured plans are required to include a minimum of 32 mandates, not including some ACA mandates.

Mandates are things such as in vitro fertilization, breast reconstruction surgery, treatment of physical complications of mastectomy, birth control, eating disorder treatment as Serious Mental Illness, Shingles Vaccine, colorectal cancer screening, organ transplant immunosuppressive drugs, etc.). Go to www.robertslayton.com/bonus to find a link to where you can find your state's mandated benefits for fully insured health plans.

Then they estimate how much healthcare will cost: network fees, access fees, pharmacy costs, prescription costs, expected claims, reinsurance for catastrophic claims, variability of government mandates (e.g., if a bill is in Congress that may impact them. They then will price in the impact), and how much profit they want to make.

If you think that the Affordable Care Act has curbed the insurance companies' profits, think again. The stock price of the five major Health Insurance carriers has gone up between 500% to over 1,000%. On January 1st, 2010, three months before the Affordable Care Act passed, United Healthcare's stock (UHC) was trading at $33 per share. On April 1st, 2021, the stock price was $390.01 per share. So $10,000 invested in their stock as of January 1, 2010 would now be worth $118,184.

Cigna's (CI) stock price on January 1st, 2010 was $33.77. On April 1st, 2021 it was $254.36. Also an amazing return.

Humana, Anthem, and Aetna all had similar increases. See **Table 1: Health Insurance Carriers Stock Value** at www.robertslayton.com/bonus to see a graph. Better yet, go out and plot the stock prices yourself.

As I'm writing this, we have a "shelter-in-place" order from our Governor due to COVID-19. The probability that health insurance premiums for fully insured plans will be going up in 2021 and maybe even 2022 is high. COVID-19 is expensive to treat (the worst cases are those on ventilators in ICU), and the insurance company will try to recoup this cost on future premiums.

Every health insurance company has stated that they will take care of all COVID-related claims (meaning no money out of the employee's pocket), but the cost WILL be rolled into renewals in future years.

In companies with less than 1000 employees, claims are more variable, meaning you typically have two good years for every bad claim year. Those companies on fully insured plans don't typically see the benefits of those two good years.

Suppose your company is on a self-insured plan (level-funded is included in this rubric). In that case, you reap some of the benefits from those two good years, which typically outweigh that one bad year because you have a cap on how much you will pay for that catastrophic claim through reinsurance (reinsurance means buying extra insurance for claims exceeding a threshold, such as $25,000 for a small company or $250,000 for a large company).

Even insurance companies buy insurance against large claims (they don't want to be stuck with a $4,000,000 bill from a provider, either).

Fully Insured Health Plans

These are the most prevalent plans in the U.S. "Fully insured" means that you pay the premium to the insurance company, and the insurance company assumes all of the risk.

If you are a small employer, your claims experience (claims incurred by your employees) is pooled with other small companies. The larger your company, the less those claims are pooled. So if you have 200 employees, your claims experience will be priced into next year's increase.

You have no control or say over the plans, the pharmacy benefit manager, quality of providers, where tests or procedures are performed, or anything else. (You may be thinking, "but I have a network.") Yes, you do, but there are good providers and bad providers within the network. Each provider has their deal with the insurance company, so you don't know what the actual provider cost will be, and you have no control over where your employees and their dependents go for service or surgeries.

It gets better, as an example, as of July 1, 2021, United Healthcare has announced that in certain states it will assess all emergency room claims and decide which are worthy of paying. This means that you, a "lay person" must determine whether you should go to the emergency room or somewhere else (i.e. Urgent Care). Anthem tried this in 2017/2018 to public outcry. Here's a link to an article from USA Today talking about it: http://bit.ly/UHCEmergencyRoom

ASO Contracts

If you are on an "Administrative Services Only" contract with an insurance company, you are still subject to the insurance company offering you plans that have their profit baked in. ASO means that the insurance company does everything but uses YOUR checkbook to pay all claims.

Think about it, would you give your company checkbook to a supplier and tell them to write their own checks? Heck, no. But it gets better, the insurance company will provide you with their accounting of the claims, but you have no cross-reference to see whether the claims costs are accurate.

Furthermore, many of the contracts with health systems have a "No Audit" clause. This means that the insurance company is NOT ALLOWED to audit claims over a certain dollar amount. THINK ABOUT THIS... The very claims that are guaranteed to have errors are the very claims they can't audit.

This is a huge issue and one of the reasons why companies are paying more than they should. We can literally take those claims and run them through our software and demonstrate how much was overpaid. BONUS: We even have a company that will go after those errors claims' cost and return between 5% to 10% of your annual premium in hard dollars to the employer. These are for things the employer should not have paid for, commonly called "overspend."

Level-Funded Health Plans

Level-funded health insurance plans are essentially self-insured plans whereby the employer pays the expected claims cost (plus 10% - 20%) to the insurance company. At the end of the year, the insurance company gives back either part or all of any leftover money in that claims fund.

If you go over the plan's expected cost of claims, then everything is fully reinsured, so you would not pay anything other than your monthly premium. This is better than a fully insured plan, but you are still subject to the insurance company designing the plan that works best for themselves and their profit, not for you and your company.

Self-Insured Health Plans

Large employers typically implement self-insured health plans.

For true self-insured health plans, you can choose the best companies and contracts for each aspect of the plan and put in more robust controls to ensure your employees are only getting the best care.

The beauty of a self-insured plan is that you can design the plan that works best for your company and employees. A properly designed plan will reduce the frequency and severity of claims and increase employees' positive health outcomes.

It's Not an All or Nothing Method

At the end of this book, everything will look great, but you'll feel overwhelmed and won't know where to start. Most employers begin with one small change, monitor it, then move to the following change once the first change demonstrates value. Being fully implemented takes time; expect it to take 3 to 5 years, especially if your group is made up of unhealthy people.

The larger your company, the better these techniques work, but we've been able to implement real change into companies as small as five employees. Of course, we can help you analyze your current plan, recommend modifications, and help implement those changes on a consulting basis.

Let's start with an overview of the cost drivers for claims. There are four main drivers [2]. They are as follows:

	Average Person	Average Family of 4
Prescription Drugs ≈	20%	11%
Hospitalization ≈	18%	31%
Outpatient Surgery ≈	31%	20%
Physician Visits ≈	28%	35%

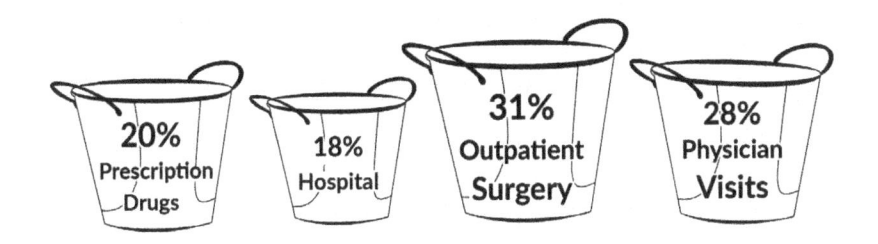

20% Prescription Drugs | **18%** Hospital | **31%** Outpatient Surgery | **28%** Physician Visits

Note that the costs vary depending upon the demographic (average single person versus family of 4). When designing health plans for companies, demographics need to be taken into account.

Later in the book, we will take each in turn and talk about what is going on, what you can do about it, a story illustrating the personal impact, and a case study showing savings.

But before we go into detail on each, we need to have a conversation about healthcare and claims in general.

The Rest of the Book

The goal is to help you understand what is happening in your health insurance contract, how to redesign your plan to reduce your (employer) cost while at the same time, providing higher quality benefits to your employees with lower deductibles/out of pocket maximums.

We will talk about the cost drivers first and how you can reduce those costs. Then we will go into the specific tactics that you can use to provide higher quality outcomes for your employees at lower cost.

UNDERSTANDING AND IMPLEMENTING THE MANIFESTO

CHAPTER 1

4 Kinds of Risk Management

NOTE: This topic will be explained in more detail with my next book. This is just an overview.

In the insurance world, the purchasing of insurance is intended to transfer the risk from yourself or your company to another entity. In this case, an insurance company or reinsurer.

That said, let's go over the four kinds of risk management and how they apply to employee benefits. As a consultant, applying risk management to your business is key to reducing the frequency and severity of claims. Jim Egerton of Business on the Board (businessontheboard.com) reminded me of this key facet during a presentation he gave discussing the risk.

Four Ways to Manage Risk

Avoid

The first way to manage risk is to AVOID it. This means making it impossible to happen. One example in the benefits world is to exclude certain extremely high-cost drugs from your formulary. By excluding the drug, you make it impossible to have it hit your plan costs.

Suppose these drugs have a patient assistance program or manufacturer coupon associated with the drug. In that case, it's possible that your employee can receive the drug at a very low cost without it impacting your bottom line.

Mitigate

The second way to manage risk is to MITIGATE it. In other words, make it less likely to happen. There are many examples of how this can be done, but a big one is to manage chronic conditions such as Diabetes.

Suppose you have a program that helps a diabetic employee stay compliant with their medications, diet, and exercise regimen. In that case, they are much less likely to have all of the secondary issues from emergency room visits to neuropathy, etc. The average cost of a compliant diabetic person is around $4,000. A non-compliant diabetic is approximately $11,000 to $15,000 [3] [4].

Another example is trying to move sick spouses and dependents off of your health plan onto their own health plan (if they work for and are offered a plan at their own place of work). Offer a program to help pay for the spouse's deductible and out of pocket if they move onto their own employer's health plan.

What's great about this is that you reduce your exposure from $30,000 or $100,000 (your individual stop loss) to just the out-of-pocket maximum ($6,000) and the only time you'd need to pay that amount is if they are sick. If a spouse moves off onto their own health plan and is healthy/doesn't use the plan, you have nothing to pay out.

Transfer

The third way to manage risk is to *transfer* it to someone else. This is precisely why you purchase insurance on your home, car, and valuables. It is also why you purchase health insurance because of the high cost of claims.

Part of the monthly premium you pay is for insuring higher-cost claims. This is done through reinsurance. Depending on how you structure your plan and your organization's size, the cost could be anywhere from 5% to over 50% of the total cost. For companies with fewer than 1000 employees, Captive plans pool the risk among companies, which dramatically reduces the cost. Captive plans also implement strategies for employers to *mitigate* risk and keep the cost of insurance low.

Accept

The fourth and final way to manage risk is to *accept* that it may happen. If you have a self-insured plan, you may have a reinsurance company apply a "laser" to your insurance. This happens if they know there is a person who will potentially cost a lot of money.

For example, a person with a brain tumor may need surgery. The laser states that they won't cover the first $X thousand dollars or may try to exclude those costs entirely. This is where a good Medical Management team comes into play.

The Medical Management team may assess the actual chance and cost of the claim and manage to a much lower number. For example, a laser stating that the employer is responsible for the first $500,000 of any brain surgery. The Medical Management team, who has been working with this individual, knows that they are not candidates for surgery and have been placed in Hospice. In this case, the company accepts the laser versus having their reinsurance premium go up dramatically or needing to shop the insurance around.

Takeaway Tips

1. Remember that buying insurance is just one way of managing risk.
2. Sometimes it is better to put programs in place to avoid or mitigate risk rather than buying insurance to cover this risk.

3. If you put into place programs to avoid or mitigate risk, your insurance costs will go down.
4. There are times when accepting the risk is okay. Just make sure you have an expert to back up your numbers to confirm the risk exposure.

CHAPTER 2

Managing Pharmacy Costs

On the average health insurance plan, around 27% of the cost is due to medications.

The cost of medications has been in the news constantly over the last few years. In my opinion, this is the wild west of the insurance world with the very entities hired to manage costs, pharmacy benefit management companies (PBMs), often driving up costs for employers instead of lowering costs. In fact, multiple entities are profiting in the pharmaceutical distribution chain that drives prescription drug costs in the US to among the highest - worldwide.

Step 1: This begins with drug manufacturers developing and testing new medications. If clinical trials go well, the drug is approved by the FDA for specific use. It is important to note that just because a new drug is approved for sale by the FDA does not mean the drug offers a clinical advantage over previously approved medications. It simply means the drug is deemed safe for human consumption and provides some level of efficacy for a targeted disease.

Below is an example showing the cost for various brand and generic diabetes medications. The brands at the top of the list all came to market long after the generics toward the bottom of the list. A goal of diabetes medications is to lower hemoglobin A1C, a blood marker for glucose control.

You can see that the cost per HgA1C reduction by one point is many times higher for the newer FDA-approved agents than the older agents toward the bottom of the list. Yet, many of the more recent brand drugs were quickly adopted by prescribers such as Januvia, even though they were less potent than other less costly diabetes agents.

Here is an example of this. Please see **Table 2: Diabetic Agents** on www.robertslayton.com/bonus for the actual chart.

Symlin is a brand-name drug that costs on average $411 per month as of this writing. It reduces the HgA1C level by 0.5 percent. Therefore the cost to reduce HgA1C by one point is $822 per month.

Januvia is $216 per month and reduces this level between 0.5 and 0.8 with an average cost to reduce the HgA1C level by 1 point of $270 per month.

Metformin ER reduces this level between 1-2 points and costs $10 per month. The average cost of reducing the HgA1C by 1 point is $5.

That's crazy! What it demonstrates is that generic drugs may work as effectively if not more effectively than the high-priced brand name drug advertised on TV.

Step 2: The drug manufacturer sets the LIST PRICE of the drug and promotes the product to doctors via drug company representatives and to the public through ads and commercials.

Step 3: Doctors prescribe the drug for FDA-approved use or for unapproved alternative conditions, called off-label prescribing.

Step 4: The patient gets their medication filled at the pharmacy.

It seems simple and straightforward enough, but what you can't see behind the scenes drives up costs for pharmaceutical therapy considerably.

What You See Is Not What You Get

There are so many hidden problems along the way from the manufacturer to dispensing pharmacy that it's hard to know where to start.

1. In line with the diabetes drug example above, two-thirds (66%) of all cancer drugs that are FDA approved show no efficacy that will help with the condition the drug was designed for [5].
2. Some doctors receive money from drug manufacturers to incentivize prescribing and peer-to-peer promotion on behalf of the manufacturer [6]. Furthermore, my personal opinion is that if a drug is new, some doctors will prescribe it instead of a well-established/tested drug to see how it works (making you the Guinea Pig).

   I had this happen to me. I had shingles, and the doctor prescribed Lyrica (back when it was new, expensive, and on TV). My personal opinion at the time was that if a drug was marketed on TV, it was too new, too expensive, and had too many side effects for me to take it. I declined the drug, and they prescribed Tramadol. The next day I was feeling better without having to be weaned off this costly drug.

   NOTE: I am not saying all doctors do this, but I guess that it happens more often than you think.

3. Many PBMs have it written into their contracts with employers that they do *not* act in a fiduciary manner for that employer. This means that they work *in their own best interest*.
4. PBMs receive large sums of money from drug manufacturers to put their drug on the formulary and even make one drug look better than other similar drugs. At first, PBMs kept the rebates from manufacturers.

Lately some of those rebates are finding their way back to employers and sometimes even employees because of the high publicity.

However, a large percentage of manufacturer payments to PBMs are not being labeled as "rebates" and are still retained by the PBMs. In exchange for this significant revenue source to PBMs, they water down or eliminate potential cost controls such as formulary restrictions, prior authorization criteria, and quantity limits.

Politicians have written bills preventing the practice of providing rebates, but those bills have gone nowhere. The latest trick by the PBMs is to pass rebates back to the plan sponsor except for rebates on "specialty drugs." Those are where the largest rebates lie.

5. Most of the large PBMs apply "spread pricing" as the basis for determining what the insurance company or employer will pay. The PBM charges the insurance company or employer (the plan sponsor) a percentage off-list price and pays the dispensing pharmacy a lesser amount. The difference between the amount paid to the pharmacy and the higher marked-up amount charged to the plan sponsor is the spread pocketed by the PBM.

That's why PBMs don't mind when the list price of a drug goes up each year. They make more money. Even the Federal Government has weighed in on spread pricing for Medicare (http://bit.ly/spreadpricing).

6. Sometimes doctors buy expensive drugs, mark up the drug's cost by up to 2000% (that's not a typo), then send the claim to the health plan (outside of the PBM). Even with the most significant discounts, 60% of a 2000% markup is still waaay too much. This is referred to as the "buy and bill" method.

You Can Do Something About Pharmacy Costs

As an employer, you CAN control your pharmacy spend. It just takes some knowledge and understanding of the market and what you can do.

1. Choose a Fiduciary PBM. To be fiduciary compliant, the PBM must have no conflicts of interest in their business model, only look out for the best interest of the plan sponsor and plan enrollees, and all financial and utilization information be fully transparent (no hidden revenue of any kind).

   They typically charge either per employee per month or per script fill for their services, and all payments received from drug manufacturers are passed through back to the plan sponsor.

2. Understand what drugs/prices you are paying for and hire a company to help manage this. If you don't get a listing of what drugs your employees take, then you

will be at the mercy of some unscrupulous doctors and drug manufacturers. We have been able to take this listing of drugs and plug it into some of our vendors' pricing. Usually, we can EASILY save 30% to 50% off of the cost of drugs without even managing the individual medications. We can prove it using actual data.
3. If you know what drugs are taken in your company, have a medical management company work with employees on what drugs they take. Sometimes it's as simple as informing an employee that there is a generic drug that has the same impact as the costly brand name drug, and if their doctor is willing to try it, it will save them $50+/month in costs.
4. Manufacturers have programs to reduce the cost of their very expensive drugs for employees (usually called a manufacturer coupon). Employees can utilize these coupons to shift the drug's cost onto the manufacturer and lower their out-of-pocket costs.

NOTE: Manufacturers have gotten wise to this and sometimes give employees a debit type card to pay for their copays or deductible associated with the drug. This means there is no benefit for the employer. The good news is that you simply write the drug out of it (no reimbursement). Then the cost of the drug is now firmly on the shoulders of the drug manufacturer. There are companies where all they do is to assist with getting expensive drugs and therapies covered with minimal employer/employee cost.

5. Use of international pharmacies. It is okay for an individual employee to use an international pharmacy to fill their medications. If they are willing, then it works really well.
6. Prescription Tourism is where an employee physically goes to another country to pick up their expensive medication (because it can't be shipped across the border). We have a company that will fly a person to San Diego, put them on a diplomatic bus to a clinic in Mexico to pick up three months' worth of medication.

   The employer pays the total costs and gives the employee spending money for a nice weekend in San Diego. Instead of spending $18,000 on three months, the cost is $6,000. It's definitely in the employer's best interest to spend $2,000 to save $10,000. BTW, it is the SAME DRUG, typically manufactured in the United States, that is shipped to Mexico. A member is not getting a lower-quality medication. It is the same medication.

7. Help employees and their families become good consumers of drugs and their costs. A communication program that helps employees ask whether there is a generic equivalent to whatever drug the doctor prescribes will go a long way to reduce the cost. Furthermore, if they simply plug the name/dosage/frequency of the drug into a website such as goodrx.com, they could see the drug's relative cost. If it is expensive, then they can ask the doctor for a generic equivalent (BTW, you can ask the doctor how much the drug costs, and usually they will say they don't know).

8. Where employees get drugs can matter significantly. So, this just came up a couple of weeks ago. A person took generic Viagra and I wanted to move them to Medicare/Supplement/Part D drug plan to save them and the company money. Looking up Part D drug plans that include this drug (sildenafil) leaves either a costly drug program or a high cost for the drug.
9. We looked up the drug on goodrx.com. The CASH PRICE of the drug at the five least expensive pharmacies is around $15 for 30 pills (Mariano's, Walmart, Osco, etc.). CVS was $331/month (btw, they just switched it to be $19 this past week). Walgreens, as of this writing, was $155. Cialis runs from $15.69 to $106.94 for 30 pills. Where you go matters.
10. For major things such as chemotherapy, it is my personal recommendation that you request a pharmacogenetic test to assure that the treatment has the potential to be effective *before* treatment begins. This test determines whether the person's body will respond to that type of drug. The more fragile the person's health, the more critical it is to perform this test.

Spending $300 on this test could save $100,000 and more importantly, the person's life.

Story

My wife was sick, so the doctor prescribed an antibiotic that cost $45 for a ten-pack of drugs. It turned out that she was allergic to this drug, so the doctor prescribed another generic antibiotic which cost $5.64. If we had asked how much the drug cost, we could have asked for a cheaper generic.

Pharmacy Case Study

Here are some real-life examples of therapy changes resulting in the same clinical outcome (helping the patient) but at a greatly reduced cost.

See **Table 3: Non-Specialty Drugs – Therapy Optimization Through Physician and Member Education** at www.robert-slayton.com/bonus

Several examples from the table are as follows:

Target Drug	Plan Paid	Alternative Drug	Plan Paid	Days Supply	Plan Savings
Pennsaid	$7,227.87	Celecoxib	$20.61	90	$7,207.26
Metformin ER	$5,532.77	Metformin HCL	$0.00	90	$5,532.77
Gastric Vraylar	$3,434.97	Aripiprazole	$17.19	90	$3,417.78

See also **Table 4: Specialty Drugs – Therapy Optimization Through the Prior Authorization Process.**

Takeaway Tips

1. Pharmacy expenses are one of the easiest places to get immediate savings from your health plan.
2. Always check out who the PBM is, and if self-insured, READ THE CONTRACT!!! If you don't know what you are looking for, there are experts who can help.

3. Manufacturers usually have programs to reduce the cost of expensive prescriptions. The key is to understand them and marry them up with your health plan such that the manufacturer pays the brunt of the costs and not the health plan.
4. If stuck with a PBM with no chance to switch, you can still layer a pharmacy savings program on top to save 10% - 50% or more off your drug spend.

CHAPTER 3

Managing Hospital Costs

Hospital costs are approximately 30% of the cost your health insurance plan incurs. Unfortunately, many surgeries are either unnecessary or could have been done at an outpatient facility.

Hospitals are the most expensive place to do anything in the United States. For instance, in the Chicagoland area, the average reimbursement to a hospital is between 264% to 500% of the Medicare price. So, if your elderly parent goes in for a procedure and is charged $10,000 and you have the same procedure with the same doctor, at the same hospital, you will be charged between $26,400 and $50,000.

BTW, that's the DISCOUNT rate. The list price (Charge Master) of this procedure (the price that a person coming in off the street with no negotiation and no insurance would pay) would typically be at least $100,000. There is a HUGE disconnect between the charge and the actual cost of the procedure (cost to the facility). If you don't believe me, just look at your next Explanation of Benefits statement from your insurance company.

What's interesting is that many of the procedures and surgeries that are done in a hospital can be done in an outpatient facility, typically with less risk of infection.

It's the Frequency and Severity of Claims

You and your employees' ultimate costs depend upon the frequency (how many) and the severity (cost) of claims. Reduce either or both and everyone saves money. So, how do you reduce these two items?

How To Reduce the Frequency of Claims: Data First

You need to understand the claims your company currently incurs (we've discussed pharmacy claims; now we'll focus on other claims). Most of the time your insurance provider will give you this data (if you are large enough). Sometimes they will charge you for it (I've seen prices range from free to over $50,000 for the privilege of them providing you with YOUR own data you should have anyway).

You can also have employees fill out Health Risk Assessments, and even get blood work done. This will be the most accurate source of determining what current and potential future conditions your employees will have.

NOTE: The data is aggregated, so the employer never knows who has what medical condition.

NOTE: I prefer much more detailed reports, but these at least give you an idea of what's going on in this group.

Top 15 Condition Report will show the top 15 overall paid expense across inpatient facility, outpatient facility, and professional settings by leading diagnostic categories

See **Table 5: Top 15 Condition Report** at www.robertslayton.com/bonus

See **Table 6: Pharmacy Example** that gives examples of pharmacy spend at www.robertslayton.com/bonus

For example, Seroquel XR Tab 300 Mg had 11 prescriptions filled with an average ingredient cost per prescription of $1,295.45.

See **Table 7: Specialty Drug Example**, includes the top spend on specialty drugs at www.robertslayton.com/bonus

For example, for this company, many of the top drugs, cost-wise were due to Fertility Treatment to the tune of $84,043 for the period.

Manage Chronic Conditions

Once you see what claims your company has had, you can look at the chronic conditions and craft a plan to help employees and their families to be compliant (think Diabetes compliance).

Proactively reach out to those employees, using a third party to help with compliance and even provide meds and other items for free. As stated previously, for diabetics, better controlled diabetes can save an average of $1,328 per person PER MONTH when looking at combined diabetes-related complications in both insured and Medicare patients [7].

With regards to Health Risk Assessments (HRA). The standard assessment tracks the top 6 chronic conditions while an extensive HRA can track up to 50. Using an HRA will also identify those who are AT RISK for developing a condition (and therefore don't show up on the claims reports). This population should be treated the same as those who have the condition as prevention is the gold standard for avoiding costs.

Require Second Opinions

Amazing as it seems, many people diagnosed with a major, life-changing condition are not automatically sent for a second opinion (or are sent to the physician's buddy vs an objective 3rd party specializing in that condition).

One example is that 28% of all cancers are misdiagnosed [8]. People are being treated for something they either don't have or are treated for the wrong kind of cancer. The treatment won't work, which means that you, the employer, continue to pay as they escalate the measures taken to save the person's life.

I've met people who have had a double mastectomy when a small lump was found in their breast. (As a corollary, *never* ask a surgeon whether surgery is the best option because they will almost always say yes. (See my dad's story later on in this book).

I also recently had a person in my office who was diagnosed with Pancreatic Cancer. When they opened him up, there was no cancer (Are you flipping kidding me?) Guess what, the insurance/employer still pays for that surgery even if it was unnecessary.

The other reason for requiring second opinions is that there are many (too many) hospitals performing procedures that are not current and not best practice treatment for that condition. Later in the book, I talk about a person who was going to have brain surgery at a local hospital. In talking with a neurosurgeon from a teaching hospital, it turned out that this particular procedure hadn't been in use for 15 years. Luckily that patient was transferred to a hospital that was using the latest technology.

Require Levels of Treatment

This can be done by contracting with a direct primary care physician, then you can have requirements for levels of treatment.

One example is that 4.5% of our national GDP is taken up by musculoskeletal disorders.

Furthermore, the leading cause of disability in the United States is due to these disorders [9]. The U.S. performs twice the number of treatments as all of the other industrialized nations with NO BETTER OUTCOMES. By extrapolation, ½ of the musculoskeletal treatments your employees are going through are not going to have a positive outcome.

By having a protocol that says a person with a musculoskeletal disorder must try physical therapy first (for those where it is appropriate, such as when a person has a "mechanical" issue – e.g., it hurts when I do X), the cost savings is dramatic. Furthermore, the employee doesn't have to undergo major surgery. This reduces the severity of claims for these types of disorders.

Move Procedures to Outpatient Surgery

There are many standard procedures that could be done in an outpatient setting that are currently being done in the hospital according to healthgrades.com [10].

Following are ten common outpatient procedures:

- Cataract Surgery
- Tendon and Muscle Repair such as a rotator cuff repair
- Small Joint Repairs, e.g. ankle surgery
- Gallbladder Removal (Cholecystectomy)
- Meniscus Repair
- Abdominal Hernia Repair

- Skin Therapy such as removal of a melanoma or acne treatment
- Lumpectomy
- Nerve Treatments such as relieving the pain in carpal tunnel syndrome
- Nose, Mouth and Pharynx Procedures such as a tonsillectomy

Outpatient facilities typically have a lower rate of infection with equal or better outcomes than an in-hospital procedure.

Use a Medical Management Company

My favorite tactic is to engage a Medical Management company that is provided with either a data stream or is the company that approves all treatments over a certain amount. They work with the member to get a second opinion, assure only the most modern up to date procedures are used, and help steer the patient to the highest quality provider.

Takeaway Tips

1. Hospitals are the MOST EXPENSIVE place to get anything done, whether it is testing, imaging, or surgery. If it is possible to get something done outside of a

hospital, then it is almost always dramatically less expensive.
2. Second opinions from experts are your friend. They will help make sure that the right diagnosis is made and the right treatment plan is created.
3. Seek out experts with DATA. The goal is the right patient is receiving the right care at the right time at the right place for the right price. Medical Management companies help with this.

CHAPTER 4

Managing Outpatient Surgery Costs

Outpatient surgery comprises approximately 20% of a health plan's spend. Unlike hospital, pharmacy, and doctor's visits, sometimes this is looked upon as a place to reduce hospital costs. So if your current spend is 40% hospital and 10% outpatient, then driving procedures that can be done in an outpatient setting into that setting will actually decrease your overall costs (with equal to better outcomes).

That said, sometimes surgery is just the wrong place to be in the first place. As you are aware, my opinion is that anyone with a major diagnosis should get an independent expert's opinion (second opinion) before proceeding with any treatment plan if possible. The chance of being forced into one course of action without confirming the diagnosis and considering multiple options is too great.

Imagine having major surgery where they prep you, put you under, and open you up, only to realize that there was no problem in the first place. This happened to a client of mine (he was diagnosed with pancreatic cancer). You still need to go through the recovery phase, not to mention the possibility of infection, potential issues with anesthesia, and other things surrounding surgery.

Some advantages of an outpatient procedure are that anesthesia doesn't last as long, it is a less invasive surgery, and there is faster recovery to home time (reducing the risk of infection). As a general rule of thumb, your Medical Management company or TPA should steer people to outpatient from the hospital unless there are secondary factors (e.g., a high-risk patient due to secondary issues that could compromise the event).

That said, what can you as an employer do to reduce this cost? Here are several options.

If You Can't Avoid Outpatient Surgery

Here are some other tips you can use to help reduce the frequency and severity of claims. Some have been mentioned earlier, but I think it's worth reading them again.

Second Opinions

Second opinions will help mitigate the risk. As with musculoskeletal disorders, surgery is recommended twice as often in the United States with no better outcomes for those disorders, so if we can get a second opinion that suggests a less invasive, less expensive alternative strategy to try first, then it should be done.

Personally, I've used acupuncture for a bulging disc (my father-in-law used it to avoid surgery on several ruptured/bulging discs himself). I sent my sister-in-law to an acupuncturist. One day we were doing dishes together when she said, "Robert, before seeing Frank [the acupuncturist], I was resigned to a life of pain with an occasional good day. Now I have good days with an occasional bad day."

In general, if you have an enlightened doctor (or have a direct primary care physician contracted for your company), they can steer a patient to a first option that avoids surgery (if possible). Please remember, we are not trying to stop people from getting the treatment they need, it's that if there is a reasonable alternative therapy that does not involve surgery, then doesn't it make sense to recommend that first?

Just like recommending a generic drug that's been in use for over 20 years instead of the new, very expensive drug that's been in use for a year or less.

You could also demand that members only use an in-network facility or use reference-based pricing (RBP - pricing based upon a multiple of the Medicare allowed rate). This reduces the cost of the surgery relative to out of network, Charge Master rate.

Behavioral Health

For many issues, especially musculoskeletal, behavioral health can play a major role in preventing unnecessary surgeries. If you require physical therapy before a person gets surgery, then there is a possibility of the person not needing the surgery.

Bundled Pricing

Make sure pricing isn't based on hospital rates due to the outpatient facility being owned by the hospital, you or your broker can facilitate arranging bundled pricing from local providers. There are some companies who have already done this which you can tap into with no extra cost other than you pay a percentage of the savings.

By the way, the cost of the bundled pricing can be over 50% less than sending a person to a surgeon where the cost hasn't been negotiated. Bundled pricing comes in at about 150% - 175% of the Medicare rate whereas network negotiated rates range from a low of 264% to over 555% of the Medicare rate (in some states 900%!!!)

The crazy thing is that the bundled pricing surgeon *has better outcomes* than most other surgeons. That's because they do a lot of procedures and have become exceedingly good at them.

Reverse Bidding

There are sites where surgeons can bid on a procedure. They are required to include their quality metrics so that the employee feels comfortable with the quality if they choose that provider.

Always Always Always Research the Provider and Facility

This also goes for hospitals. The top doctors/surgeons are almost always the least expensive. They typically do dozens of surgeries every week, use higher quality materials (e.g. titanium knee facings), have lower infection/recidivism rates, and a smoother overall process. A surgery done properly once means that there are no extra, unexpected, expenses.

A friend of mine went in for back surgery (5 weeks ago from this writing). They were supposed to remove one disc (discectomy). She didn't look at the objective metrics of the surgeon but went solely on the recommendation of her family doctor.

After the first surgery, she had to go back in because she was leaking spinal fluid. Second major surgery, couldn't find it. Third surgery, nothing. Fourth surgery, they finally found and fixed it. So, if that surgeon were 1/3 the cost, they had four surgeries. But the surgeon wasn't cheap. The worst part is that my friend was subjected to 4 surgeries, and put her life on the line and on hold for weeks due to the quality of the doctor.

Sometimes stuff happens. By using the best surgeon, the chances of it happening are greatly reduced.

While the surgeon and their staff are most important, if the facility where the procedure is being done is not up to snuff, then it can also be a place for potential problems.

Websites to Review Doctors and Hospitals

Here are some links to websites to help you start the process of checking on the quality of the doctor or facility.

Peer-Reviewed

The following sites rely on members' reviews. This means they aren't as accurate with regards to actual quality metrics.

However, It is a starting point and usually, the site will say whether there have been any sanctions against a doctor.

Healthgrades.com

Ratemds.com

Vitals.com

Externally Reviewed

Castleconnolly.com lists doctors and practices who have been nominated and gone through a vetting process on key quality metrics. The downside is that there are very few doctors/groups listed.

NCQA.org looks at the report cards. Again, this is a site where doctors, health plans, organizations, and hospitals can buy into to be a part of the program. In my opinion, only the most on-the-ball doctors/organizations will be part of it. I'm not sure about the health plans (insurance products listed).

Leapfrog publishes a Hospital Survey that reports data on each individual facility rather than at the hospital system level (for example, data on Central DuPage Hospital versus data on Northwestern Medical System in Illinois). It gives the most detailed review of the facility in 4 different areas, Infections, Problems with Surgery, Practices to Prevent Errors, Safety Problems, and Doctors, Nurses & Hospital Staff.

This program is voluntary, so not all facilities are included (but most are across the United States). Here is a sample (below) from their web page on infections for a sample hospital. For more information go here: http://bit.ly/leapfroghospitalsurvey. More information on the Survey can be found here:

http://bit.ly/LeapfrogHospitalSurveyInfo

They also have another program called "Hospital Safety Grade" which is a website where they create a composite Patient Safety rating from publicly available data (much of it from CMS). For more information, go here: http://bit.ly/HospitalSafetyGrade

Both are fully transparent and free to the public. See **Table 8**: **LeapFrog Group Hospital Safety Grade Example** to see how the graphic looks. www.robertslayton.com/bonus

Takeaway Tips

1. Always seek second opinions if surgery is recommended. Many times therapy can resolve the problem.
2. Seek out the highest performing doctors if you need surgery. My mom's knee replacement became infected and needed to be removed, then antibiotic treatment followed, putting the knee back in (a 12-week process for this mid 80-year-old, who still plays golf). The doctor we chose had a score of 98.1 out of 100 (the

highest score I've seen). The surgery was done and she's doing remarkably well for her age.
3. There are programs that will do bundled pricing for procedures. This usually dramatically reduces the cost while maintaining a high quality. Seek out these programs.

CHAPTER 5

Managing Physician Visits

Twenty percent of healthcare spending comes through physician visits. To tell the truth, usually the higher the frequency of visits to a family doctor, the less likely that a person will pass through to the higher cost services. Furthermore, around 40% of the transactions within a health plan are doctor visits. The TPA (the company or division that administers the plan) spends a lot of resources in managing these (doing the eligibility, payments, EOBs, etc).

The family doctor (and OB/GYN) is on the front lines for medical care. In the medical group that my doctor belongs to, family doctors are given bonuses to keep them because medical groups realize that they are the avenue to the higher cost/ higher profit procedures/treatments.

Your doctor will recommend testing, therapy, or a specialist for a possible condition. By controlling the steerage (steering a member to a particular facility or doctor), the medical group makes more money. Conversely, if you control the steerage (by directly contracting a doctor, utilizing a medical management company, or third-party administrator who understands what you are trying to do) then your costs go down.

Here are some ways to reduce costs/make this more effective:

Direct Contracting

Directly contract with a doctor where the doctor is compensated not on how many patients they see, but rather the quality and outcomes of the patients. With direct contracting, the employer agrees to pay a flat amount per month for the doctor to see its members.

The doctor then typically spends around 30 minutes with each patient instead of the average of 6 to 12 minutes. The longer period of time allows a deeper understanding of the issue and new alternatives such as diet/exercise instead of medication to be discussed. Members are more likely to follow the recommendations because they have a stronger relationship with their doctor.

The directly contracted doctor means that they are not beholden to a larger medical group to refer members to. They can steer patients to less invasive, lower-cost treatments first rather than having a really expensive surgery/medication be the first recommendation.

The employer can also keep metrics on diagnoses and recommendations to assure the doctor is following the philosophy of the group. Note that the doctor does have the final say for the patient, but if a trend is identified that the doctor is sending all people reporting back pain to a particular surgeon before physical therapy is tried, then something can be done about it.

Doctors love these arrangements because they can just practice medicine without worrying about billing, insurance, or getting paid. They can also work a 40-hour work week. The next time you are with your primary care doctor, ask them how many hours per week they work. My guess is most will say 60+ just to make enough to pay all the bills (medical billers, insurance, overhead, etc).

By the way, throw in free generic medications if you can. This incentivizes the doctor to provide lower-cost medications and members to be more compliant. According to the CDC 20% of prescriptions are never filled and among those that are filled, approximately 50% are taken incorrectly. Nonadherence costs have grown to between $100 - $300 billion of U.S. health care dollars spent each year [11].

Set Up a Clinic

We have programs to help either larger employers (500 or more employees) or a group of employers (with at least 500 total employees – such as in several office buildings) set up their own clinic. A nurse practitioner or doctor is hired directly and compensated by the employer or group.

You can typically entice one of the best doctors in the area to work for the clinic because they now don't need to worry about contracts, billers, insurance, overhead, or anything else. They can work a normal schedule, spend more time with patients, and still make more money.

Ask for A Rate Reduction from the TPA

If you do one of the above, then you can ask for a lower rate because you are removing 40% of the cost from the TPA's plate. That reduces the overall cost of the program. In the long run, it will save you a bundle.

Telemedicine

Telemedicine is something most standard insurance companies have already added and with the Coronavirus, it has expanded exponentially. If not, then run, don't walk, to get a telemedicine program implemented. One pro is that you can contract either with a very low monthly per employee per month rate for zero cost visits. This includes unlimited doctor consultations or you can pay a lower per member cost (as of this writing, I've seen around $40/visit).

In all cases it is cheaper than visiting a doctor in their office. Another pro is that employees don't lose a ½ day of work going to see their primary doctor. The consultation, diagnosis, and treatment can be done right from the employee's desk. Many times, the doctor will say they can finish out the day and a medication (e.g. antibiotic) will be waiting for them at their local pharmacy.

The con is that it is not your doctor. They will take a medical history, but if you have a complex medical condition, make sure the doctor on the phone realizes this.

About 70% of the time the doctor can diagnose and come up with a treatment plan over the phone or video call. The other 30% see them referring the member to their own doctor for further investigation.

NOTE: There are newer programs called "Virtual Direct Primary Care Physicians" – VDPC. These are virtual doctors who become your primary care doctor. This means that any time you have an issue, you talk to YOUR doctor, not just whoever is available. Expect this to grow dramatically over the next several years.

Overall, you will save money and have more present employees by implementing this simple extra.

EAP and Mental Health

This may not fit in this topic, but it is vitally important that you provide support to your employees in the form of an employee assistance program (EAP) and even stronger mental health programs that are usually available.

An EAP typically provides three to five calls or visits with a counselor to help with the vicissitudes of life (stress at work/home, moving, elderly parents, issues with children, financial problems, being upset with this author, etc.). They will help to either resolve a simple/finite issue or refer to local resources for more support. The cost for this is either included with some forms of insurance (e.g. if you have group disability insurance) or it can be bought inexpensively.

Something newer has been tele-mental-health. A person is assigned a counselor to help them work through the issues they are having. Program details vary, but my philosophy is that if you can help an employee deal with their life, then they will be a much more engaged and loyal employee for you.

Many people skip counseling because of either the cost or the stigma associated with it. By providing tele-mental-health, the person can get the help they need in the privacy of their own home for little to no cost.

NOTE: I am passionate about this for many reasons, including the fact that I have a Master's Degree in Counseling and was even a Licensed Professional Counselor before pursuing the field of insurance (where I still use the skills every day).

Takeaway Tips

1. Fee-for-service is an old model that rewards the worst doctors (every time you see a doctor, they get paid). Consider, instead, contracting with doctors for a flat monthly fee per member/family.
2. Telemedicine has taken off during the COVID world and is a great resource to help with standard problems like colds, minor problems such as acne, sprained ankle, etc.
3. Mental health is incredibly important and can drive the utilization of the medical system. Make sure to offer at least an EAP if not lower-cost counseling services to employees.

CHAPTER 6

How Taking on Risk can Reduce Cost

Risk is NOT a bad thing. As a matter of fact, if done correctly, it will dramatically reduce your costs without creating undue exposure. Let's look at accepting some of the risk.

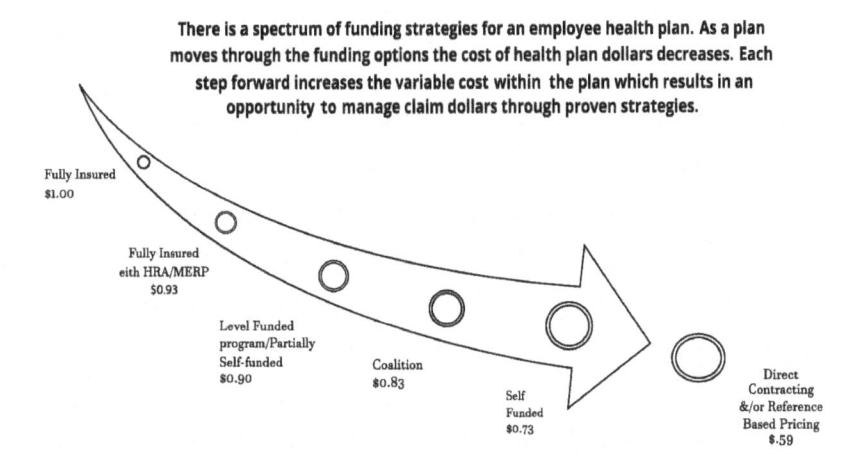

There is a spectrum of funding strategies for an employee health plan. As a plan moves through the funding options the cost of health plan dollars decreases. Each step forward increases the variable cost within the plan which results in an opportunity to manage claim dollars through proven strategies.

Fully Insured
$1.00

Fully Insured
eith HRA/MERP
$0.93

Level Funded
program/Partially
Self-funded
$0.90

Coalition
$0.83

Self
Funded
$0.73

Direct
Contracting
&/or Reference
Based Pricing
$.59

These are average numbers. Sometimes we've been able to save a company 40% by moving from one risk level to the next level, sometimes it doesn't work immediately. That's why data is so important.

Fully Insured Plans

The company takes on zero risk. They pay the premium and the insurance company takes care of the rest. Employees love these plans because they receive a card where they can go to almost any doctor or hospital and have no cap of expenses for themselves other than their deductible/out-of-pocket maximum. Picture it like giving an employee a credit card with no constraints on how to spend the money and no repercussions however they use it. It is the highest cost kind of health insurance.

Fully Insured with an HRA/MERP

For those employers who want to dip their toes into the waters of accepting some risk, there is a strategy whereby you choose a health insurance plan with a very high deductible and low premium, and then buy down that high deductible to a reasonable level (or the company's original level).

For example, let's say that your current monthly premium is $100,000 for a $1500 deductible plan for 100 employees. If you choose a $6000 deductible plan, your premium is $70,000. Then you layer in a health reimbursement arrangement or medical expense reimbursement plan of $4500 per employee. This means that if the employee spends more than $1500 on their deductible, the company will pick up 80% of the balance between $1501 and $6000. Here are the numbers from my software that calculates claims and management costs:

Original Plan before implementing the HRA

100 Total enrolled employees.

New Plan with the HRA

A $6000 deductible for one person (employee only), then pays at 100% of any excess charges. For employees with dependents, then it is a $12,000 deductible before paying 100% of any excess charges.

NOTE: If an individual reaches the individual maximum, then they do not need to meet the family maximum (this is called an embedded deductible/out of pocket maximum).

Plan Design Using the HRA

The new plan includes doctor and prescription copays which are paid as usual.

If an employee or dependent reaches $1500, then the plan will pay 80% of the remaining deductible. This means that the plan pays $3,600 and the employee pays another $900.

Double these numbers for 2+ people maxing out the insurance within a family.

The total amount an employee will pay in a year is $2,400 and the maximum a family will pay in a year is $4,800. This is less than their original plan.

Plan Costs and Savings

The total expected claims plus management cost is $5,729.28 per month or $68,751.36 per year.

Monthly premium savings is $30,000 or $360,000 per year.

Net savings is $360,000 - $68,751.36 = $291,248.64 per year.

Let's double the expected claims costs to $137,502.72. The net annual savings is still $222,497.28.

Will you get pushback from employees? Yes, a little, because now they have to submit claims to the HRA vendor. It's an extra step they have to do in order to be reimbursed for any expenses over the $1500 deductible.

Level-Funded/Partially Self-Funded Plan

We have already described these plans at the beginning of the book. Here are several key points.

1. The cost of the plan is based upon the health of the group. If the group is generally healthy, they will save between 10% - 20% from a fully insured plan.
2. You receive claims data that you can take action on. If you have more than 20 enrolled employees, you'll be able to see the kinds of claims that employees are incurring. That way you can do communication campaigns to minimize higher cost, unnecessary claims, such as going to the emergency room instead of urgent care/telemedicine.
3. Not all of the state mandates apply to you because this is considered an ERISA (I won't get into this now) plan (so based more on Federal mandates than state mandates).
4. If there is an ACA Health Insurer tax reinstated, then these policies are exempt.

Example

I took a company with 36 employees from a $42,000/month renewal down to $23,000 with a level-funded, high deductible plan. I then layered in a MERP (a "flavor" of HRA) to match their original plan benefit to benefit. Included a Medical Management company, telemedicine and benefit concierge service and saved them $180,000 the first year, $150,000 the second year, and it will be over $100,000 in the third year (with 41 employees now).

Coalition

Also known as a Captive, this is simply putting together a group of similar companies to partially self-insure the reinsurance costs. Let's say you have a regular level-funded or self-insured plan. Your stop loss may be $30,000 (if an individual has claims more than $30,000, then reinsurance kicks in and pays 100% of all claims above this number).

With a coalition, you'd keep the same $30,000 stop loss feel, but the coalition would be responsible for a middle layer (for example between $30,000 and $230,000). All claims above this amount are fully reinsured (at a lower premium due to the economies of scale of buying as a group of employers). It is necessary for coalitions to be fully funded so for many captives, there can be a collateral amount (each employer puts in $X into the fund) in order to receive the upside.

The nice part is that you only need to put in the capital once (as long as claims run as expected) and you can continue to receive a return. At the end of the year, if claims were less than expected, the employer may receive money back on that number (such as 10% return on your total stop loss premium).

Coalitions allow employers to receive additional upside when they begin addressing their claims without taking the risks and variability of further self-insuring on their own. Because you have many people in the coalition, the law of large numbers helps to make claims/expenses more predictable. If the coalition requires use of the principles found in this book, then it is possible to have a well performing captive and receive those returns on an annual basis.

Self-Funded

We've already discussed self-funded plans. This is what large employers typically do, but even they get stuck with crappy components, just see what happened to the City of Rockford in Illinois when they chose one of the largest PBMs to manage their prescription drugs. Here's a link to one of the articles: http://bit.ly/CityofRockfordPBMLawsuit Feel free to Google more on the case.

Direct Contracting and/or Reference-Based Pricing

This is minimizing risk by reducing the cost of care (severity of claims).

[We've already talked about] Direct Contracting is where you negotiate directly with doctors, usually paying a flat rate or monthly rate for access to them and negotiating a bundled, all-in rate with hospitals for common procedures. Both doctors and hospitals like these arrangements because of the increased business they receive.

NOTE: Only negotiate with the BEST doctors and the hospitals with the BEST scores for the procedures you are looking to cover.

Reference Based Pricing (RBP) is where you only pay a multiple of the Medicare approved amount. Most networks pay a discounted rate off the Charge Master rate (the highest rate the health provider charges). RBP starts with Medicare as a starting point and works its way up. Usually paying between 125% - 200% of the Medicare approved amount for whatever needs to be done.

The reason why this works is that network negotiated rates usually fall between 264% and 550% of the Medicare rate. As stated earlier in the book, this means if your elderly parent gets a knee replacement from Dr. Smith at Anytown Hospital for $10,000, then if you got the EXACT same procedure from the same doctor at the same hospital. Your cost would be between $26,400 and $55,000.

RBP has the potential of causing a lot of noise due to doctors and hospitals refusing to serve members (this doesn't happen too often in most places in the country) or the doctors/hospitals balance billing the member for the difference between payment and the bill (all good RBP programs indemnify members against this balance billing, but it is still stressful for the member as they are being threatened for non-payment by the medical office).

Takeaway Tips

1. Realize that since insurance is purely a transfer of risk, that managing your plan's risk can result in dramatic savings which can translate into better health plans for employees (e.g. a $0 deductible health plan) while at the same time reducing the cost for the employer.
2. There are many ways of managing risk and one of the best ways is to start small and have a 3 – 5 year plan to move to managing more risk.
3. Remember that the senior executive must be the champion of change as any time you make changes to a health plan, there will be push back and "noise" from members.

CHAPTER 7

The Importance of Second Opinions and Medical Management

A client related a story to me about his brother, who had an accident and suffered a brain injury. The hospital was going in to operate on him within the day. My client had a close friend who was a top neurosurgeon at the University of Wisconsin Madison Hospital, so he called to get a second opinion on the surgery.

After sending up the records, there was a long pause on the other end of the phone until the neurosurgeon replied, "That surgery hasn't been done in over 15 years. Please remove him from that hospital and get him up here now."

Luckily, my client "had a friend" who happened to provide exactly the second opinion needed, and it was timely. His brother came through the surgery (the one his friend suggested) and fully recovered.

I'd like to believe that this was a rare occasion, but unfortunately, it happens more than we'd like to admit. Some doctors and surgeons don't always keep up with the latest advances in their field, so keep doing what they have always done.

This is why it is important to have a combination of medical management and second opinions. Medical Management because they keep track of the best practices for diagnosis and treatment and can help guide a person to talk to their doctor about choosing the treatment most suited for themselves. Second opinions are important because the current doctor may not be up on the latest breakthroughs in the industry, so sending the records to someone who keeps up on those breakthroughs means a higher probability of correct diagnosis and treatment.

Another thought: If you can get a team approach to your condition, diagnosis, and treatment, then you are much more likely to have the correct diagnosis and treatment plan. This is why places such as the Mayo Clinic in Minnesota and Rush Hospital in Chicago are successful. They have a group of doctors look at the data from the viewpoint of their specialty and render an opinion. Next, the doctors sit in a room together to make sure all work towards the benefit of the patient.

Here's another example. My mom woke up in excruciating pain one morning. She could barely get up and walk and couldn't sleep at night. She went to her doctor who referred her to a back specialist and scheduled an Xray/MRI a week out. So, for the next week, my mom couldn't sleep, move, and barely ate. Then it was another week before the specialist got back to her.

My brother finally had enough. He called in a favor and had her in at Rush within two days. The beauty of Rush in Chicago is that they do the testing, diagnosis, and treatment plan all within the same day (it may be an extremely long day).

They did the testing; a group of doctors sat around a table and discussed their findings and came up with a treatment plan. She needed a disc fusion. This was scheduled a couple of days later. The medical management company reviewed the surgeon and he scored 94 out of a possible 100 (excellent). The surgery was done successfully.

One drawback was that she "waited" so long before getting the surgery done, that her right leg muscles were out of whack, so the recovery took a lot longer than normal (she needed a walker at first). This was due to the first set of doctors not taking her pain/problems seriously enough to make her a high priority. Her muscles both atrophied on one side and strengthened a little bit on the other side because of her trying to compensate for the pain.

According to a 2017 study [12], 88% of patients who visited the Mayo Clinic for a second opinion on a complex procedure go home with a new or refined diagnosis, changing their care plan and potentially saving their lives.

If you don't have a medical management company available, then ask for a second opinion. If that doesn't seem to be working then you can ask what studies the treatment plan is based upon. This gives you an indication as to whether the doctor truly is up to date. If the doctor blows you off, then you may want to consider a different doctor.

Takeaway Tips

1. We've talked about the importance of second opinions both in this chapter and in previous ones. The key is to get a second opinion from a specialist in that area preferably not associated with the same practice (meaning that the specialist is incentivized to confirm the diagnosis).
2. If possible, a multi-disciplinary second opinion is best. The Mayo Clinic (and Rush Hospital in Chicago) are known for doing this. You arrive in the morning for testing, then when the results come back, a number of doctors in different specialties sit around a table and discuss your case. That way nothing is missed from diagnosis to treatment plan.

CHAPTER 8

Be Your Own Advocate

Around five years ago, my father (age 78 at the time) was diagnosed with Stage 1 aggressive bladder cancer. The recommendation at the time was to have a cystectomy (bladder removal surgery).

Here's how I imagine the conversation between my dad and the surgeon went.

Surgeon: You have stage 1 bladder cancer. It is aggressive, so we recommend a radical cystectomy.

My dad: So, what does this mean?

Surgeon: We remove your bladder, prostate, and seminal vesicles and fashion a new bladder from your intestine. You should be able to urinate again (because we'd do a neobladder reconstruction). Of course, since it is radical surgery, there are the risks of bleeding, blood clots, and infection. Furthermore, after it is done, due to what we removed, there could be dehydration, electrolyte abnormalities, urinary tract infection, and a possible blockage of either your intestine or urinary tubes.

My dad: Nah, I don't think so. If the good Lord wants to take me, I'm good.

Surgeon: So, you don't want to go ahead?

My dad: Nope.

Surgeon: Oh.

What they did instead was to use in-bladder chemotherapy (since they can reach the bladder directly without being invasive), scraped the lining and took a little bit of the wall out. In the end, he's been cancer-free for five years with a much better quality of life and much more likely to live longer than if he would have had that surgery.

Lesson

My personal opinion is to never ask a surgeon whether surgery is the best option. They will almost always say yes (and believe it). Get a second opinion and all options before committing to one course of treatment, especially if it is radical/major.

If you are able, look at the research surrounding the treatment to see if the studies were done on people of similar age, gender, and ethnic descent. This gives you extra information as to whether the treatment would work for you.

CHAPTER 8: BE YOUR OWN ADVOCATE

If you are a 55-year-old black male and the studies were done on 22-year-old white females, then there is a disconnect. The studies may not have your exact demographic, but the closer it is, the better. Review the controversy surrounding studies using statins to reduce cholesterol. The vast majority of those studies were done on men, not women, so it was much harder to get a read on whether they are as effective with women.

Takeaway Tips

1. Be your own advocate.
2. If you can't be your own advocate, find someone who will be. My friend kept a spreadsheet on her dad's very complex situation that included every diagnosis, treatment plan, prescription, and doctor/nurse to render any of them. She saved her dad's life a couple times by countermanding a treatment that was different than what was agreed to.

Book Summary

The goal of this book is to help you understand what is happening in your health insurance contract, how to redesign your plan to reduce your (employer) cost while at the same time, providing higher quality benefits to your employees with lower deductibles/out of pocket maximums.

In this book we learned that the vast majority of health insurance has nothing to do with insurance. Most deals with administering the plan and paying for claims. The difference between a self-insured health plan and one by the "big 5 insurers" is that you have control over administration, the cost of claims, and how you pay claims. If you are on a fully insured plan, then you are at the mercy of a system set up to make sure the insurance company makes a profit (and satisfies its stockholders) versus reducing the frequency and cost of claims and keeping those savings within your company.

How is this done? Well, this handbook gives you a head start on the major components of a health plan and how to make a difference in each of these components. As always, my suggestion is to use a person who understands this and can connect you to the best solutions. If you'd like a consultation, go to www.robertslayton.com/contactus to set up a time to talk.

Consolidated Listing of All Tips

Below is a summary of all of the tips from each chapter.plus 10 Bonus Tips! That way you don't need to hunt through the book for these recommendations.

Chapter 1 – 4 Kinds of Risk Management

1. Remember that buying insurance is just ONE way of managing risk.
2. Sometimes it is better to put programs in place to avoid or mitigate risk rather than buying insurance to cover this risk.
3. If you put into place programs to avoid or mitigate risk, your insurance costs will go down.
4. There are times when accepting the risk is okay. Just make sure you have an expert to back up your numbers to confirm the risk exposure.

Chapter 2 – Managing Pharmacy Costs

1. Pharmacy expenses are one of the easiest places to get immediate savings from your health plan.
2. Always check out who the PBM is, and if self-insured, read the contract!!! If you don't know what you are looking for, there are experts who can help.
3. Manufacturers usually have programs to reduce the cost of expensive prescriptions. The key is to

understand them and marry them up with your health plan such that the manufacturer pays the brunt of the costs and not the health plan.

Chapter 3 – Managing Hospital Costs

1. Hospitals are the most expensive place to get anything done, whether it is testing, imaging, or surgery. If it is possible to get something done outside of a hospital, then it is almost always dramatically less expensive.
2. Second opinions from experts are your friend. They will help make sure that the right diagnosis is made and the right treatment plan is created.
3. Seek out experts with data. The goal is the right patient is receiving the right care at the right time at the right place for the right price. Medical Management companies help with this.

Chapter 4 – Managing Outpatient Surgery Costs

1. Always seek second opinions if surgery is recommended. Many times therapy can resolve the problem.
2. Seek out the highest performing doctors if you need surgery. My mom's knee replacement became infected and needed to be removed, then antibiotic treatment, then putting the knee back in (a 12-week process for this mid 80-year-old who still plays golf). The doctor we chose had a score of 98.1 out of 100 (the highest score I've seen). So far so good (she's in her 6th week).

3. There are programs that will do bundled pricing for procedures. This usually dramatically reduces the cost while maintaining high quality. Seek out these programs.

Chapter 5 – Managing Physician Visits

1. Fee-for-service is an old model that rewards the worst doctors (every time you see a doctor, they get paid). Consider, instead, contracting with doctors for a flat monthly fee per member/family.
2. Telemedicine has taken off during the COVID world and is a great resource to help with standard problems like colds, minor problems such as acne, sprained ankle, etc.
3. Mental health is incredibly important and can drive the utilization of the medical system. Make sure to offer at least an EAP if not lower-cost counseling services to employees.

Chapter 6- How Taking on Risk Can Reduce Cost

1. Realize that since insurance is purely a transfer of risk, that managing your plan's risk can result in dramatic savings which can translate into BETTER health plans for employees (e.g. a $0 deductible health plan) while at the same time reducing the cost for the employer.
2. There are many ways of managing risk and one of the best ways is to start small and have a 3 – 5 year plan to move to manage more risk.
3. Remember that the senior executive MUST be the champion of change as any time you make changes

to a health plan, there will be push back and "noise" from members.

Chapter 7 – The Importance of Second Opinions and Medical Management

1. We've talked about the importance of second opinions both in this chapter and other chapters. The key is to get a second opinion by a specialist in that area preferably not associated with the same practice (meaning that the specialist is incentivized to confirm the diagnosis).
2. If possible, a multi-disciplinary second opinion is best. The Mayo Clinic (and Rush Hospital in Chicago) are known for doing this. You arrive in the morning for testing, then when the results come back, a number of doctors in different specialties sit around a table and discuss your case. That way nothing is missed from diagnosis to treatment plan.

Chapter 8 – Be Your Own Advocate

1. BE YOUR OWN ADVOCATE.
2. If you can be your own advocate, find someone who will be. My friend kept a spreadsheet on her dad's very complex situation that included every diagnosis, treatment plan, prescription, and doctor/nurse to render any of them. She saved her dad's life a couple times by countermanding a treatment that was different than what was agreed to.

10 Bonus Tips

If you don't have time to read the whole book, then consider these 10 bonus tips:

1. Health Insurance costs are manageable. You can reduce the cost of your health insurance regardless of whether your HR or Broker says it can't be done.
2. You do not manage health insurance costs by shopping the market for insurance providers. Spreadsheeting (we call it spread-shitting) is a thing of the past for mid to larger employers.
3. Most brokers do not know how to manage these costs, so seek out an Adviser to evaluate your existing plan and make recommendations. Your current broker can manage the plan you choose, but if they don't know how to design the plan that puts you and your employees into the center of it, then find an Adviser who can.
4. There are specific things you can do now to reduce your costs without changing your health plan. Two examples are layering a specialty pharmacy program on top of your existing prescription drug plan and implementing a program where people with musculoskeletal issues must get a second opinion and try physical therapy first before surgery.
5. Usually, the larger brokers will not be able to implement significant changes to your health plan. They are not allowed by their owners because it would cut into

their compensation. They may say they can do some of these items, but are unwilling to put a performance guarantee on it. For example, for some programs I will guarantee a reduction in costs, or else I don't get paid a dime or I take a portion of the savings.
6. The highest-quality doctors/surgeons are typically the least expensive. Also, within a hospital, there are excellent doctors/surgeons who charge much less than other doctors/surgeons at the same hospital.
7. Data is your friend. It will help you manage your health care spend, identify places where you can positively impact your employees' health outcomes, and reduce the frequency and severity of claims.
8. The big insurance carriers, inside the black box, do exactly the same things as purely self-insured plans. The difference is that when an insurance carrier designs a plan, they design it to make a profit for them. When you design a plan, you design it to reduce the cost for you and increase the quality of care for your employees. This sounds difficult but is easier than you think IF you use the right consultant.
9. You don't have to do everything at once. You can start with one change. For example, layering a specialty pharmacy on top of your existing plan.
10. Make sure you choose a broker who understands these principles. You can try yourself or have your existing broker implement these ideas, but if they haven't vetted the resources, then things may not work out

as well as you'd hope. One easy way to tell is if they downplay the value of these options or say something negative about them, then they are the wrong broker for exploring/implementing these principles.

Bonus Material

Epilogue - Managing the Rapid Pace of Change

Muscle Testing

One method of tapping into your true "gut reaction"/intuition when faced with a decision is this:

Make a circle on one hand by pressing the tip of your thumb and forefinger against each other. Then with the other hand, put that thumb and forefinger inside the first circle and press them against each other, creating two interlocking circles.

Next, keeping them tightly interlocked so the resistance is strong, try pulling the circles apart. That's your break strength. The next step is to ask two opposing questions, one at a time, such as: "Should I not pursue this opportunity?" and try breaking the circles apart while doing so. Then ask, "Should I keep things the same?" and pull your hands apart again. Whichever pull is harder to make while pulling your fingers apart is the one your intuition is saying you should follow. This is often referred to as "muscle testing."

You can test it using a basic statement like, "I am X years old" using your actual age. Then "I am Y years old" using the wrong age. You'll immediately see the difference in your responses. You can also have fun with this with your kids.

A different technique is to work with another person and have them raise their dominant arm straight out to the side. Tell them to resist as you ask them a question or make a statement that they're pondering and then push down on the arm. Have them notice how much resistance they felt as you make a mental note of it, too. Then ask them an opposite question or make a contrasting statement and do the same thing. Whichever answer results in making it harder to push the arm down is the direction to follow. In other words, their strength in holding steadfast is the determinator of what's in their highest good.

As for kids, if they want to eat junk food (e.g., a bag of chips), have them hold the bag over their heart with their non-dominant hand while putting their other arm out to the side. Then push down on their dominant arm. Next, give them something healthy such as a banana. Do the same thing and watch their/your reaction. Many adults use this form of muscle testing to decide upon the healthiest supplements or foods for themselves. You can use it for many purposes, bearing in mind that the body doesn't lie.

One Last Comment

If you use the energy approach/muscle testing above and you do not experience any strong response, then you need to rethink either the opportunity, question, or recraft the opportunity to make it more compelling.

Adaptation

The pace of change is accelerating at an astonishing speed. Gone are the days where it took several months or even up to a year to study a market and come up with a positive response. In the era of instant government overthrow via Twitter, we have less time to analyze a problem or opportunity before we are forced to respond.

The question is how to identify these items quickly and then gather enough information in order to make a good response (versus reacting). Just refer to the Coronavirus outbreak we lived through (which I am living through as I write this from an upstairs bedroom).

Kudos To You

If you are reading this book, chances are that you are successful. Let's be realistic, who in their right mind would be interested in reading a book like this unless they had either a vested interest due to their position in an organization or has an impact amongst others for this topic.

This means that you've been successful in navigating hundreds of changes in your organization and life. Take a moment to pat yourself on your back. You may not realize it, but you are AWESOME!

Identifying Issues and Opportunities

Personally, I spend several hours a day monitoring the world revolving around health care and insurance. High on my list is how the government is currently viewing my industry, who the players are, and how it may shape up in the future. State issues matter along with new players in the benefits space. Those players are the ones I talk to on a weekly basis to see how they fit into the new benefits space. They must add value to the NextGen model of care or else it's a polite, "no thank you" and I move one.

The reason why so much time is spent is that I need the ability to pivot before the large players even realize there's been a change. Because of this ability, I've been able to capture more business and help more people.

Most likely you have a routine you follow to do the same thing. If you don't, my suggestion is to start, even if it is 1 hour per week. Here are my tips to help.

1. Find daily or weekly newsletters that talk about your industry on a regulatory basis. Understand that there are right-leaning, left-leaning, and occasionally central-leaning viewpoints. If you can't find one of the central-leaning newsletters, then subscribe to both the right and left-leaning newsletters (if you have time, you should subscribe anyway). It's amazing how a person's view shades the topic. It will be made clear when you read both right and left viewpoints on the same topic.

Think about those people who only watch FoxNews or CNBC without the benefit of seeing the other side of the story. They will stake their life on that viewpoint without regard to the reality of the situation. Napoleon Hill once said that there are 3 sides to every story. Your side, their side, and the right side (what actually happened). The closer we can get to what actually happened or is happening, the better our ability to discern what is going on and respond effectively.

2. Seek out opinions that are opposite from your own. I love talking to Illinois Senator Linda Holmes. We are at opposite ends of the political spectrum. When I ask her opinion on a topic, it is usually not a perspective I've thought of before so it forces me to stretch my mind to encompass her viewpoint and hopefully give me a much better idea of the issue being discussed. We almost never meet in the middle, but it gives me an appreciation of what other people are thinking.

3. Talk to your clients and prospects as often as possible. Sometimes you can identify trends that are not talked about in the media. For example, as much as former President Trump talked about how good the economy was, some of my high-tech companies have been decimated by the restrictions on H1b visas.

Yes, you can make the argument that there are plenty of people legally able to work in the United States, but it just isn't the case. These high-tech companies pay a prevailing wage (way over $100,000/year) for this talent, but they can't find enough quality talent to fill the needs of their clients. Remember, it takes not just money, but the talent needs to want to work in that industry/work for that company.

4. Seek out tangential industries. I keep track of the train wreck that is the publish or perish world of academia. Up until recently, it is estimated that at least 30% of all studies that reported a positive significant result were either manipulated or can't be replicated. Think about the impact of this on the health care world. Imagine doctors relying on these studies to diagnose and prescribe treatment for the population. If you wonder why we as a society are getting sicker in some areas, then just look here. In my prior book, I used the statistic that two-thirds of all cancer drugs approved for use have *no evidence* that they work [13].

   I happened to have taken classes in experimental design after college, so I am familiar with how to structure studies properly and the kinds of statistical analyses available to prove that the result is significant.

5. Seek out unique people—people who are different from you—who might be considered by some to be woo-woo. In reality, these may simply be people trained in alternative and holistic healing therapies, or ones who rely upon their intuition more than the average left-brained person.

We always need to expand our worldview and this helps. This outreach will result in all kinds of new insights. What I do is to take a book off the sorting shelf at the library. I figure if it is good enough for someone else to read, then I'll read it.

How about teen romance novels? Yup. How to learn a foreign language fluently in 3 months, check. Heck, I had heard about this book kids were loving years ago, so I checked out *Harry Potter and the Sorcerer's Stone* [14] just after it was published and was hooked to the point that my wife pre-ordered the book at 7 to be picked up at midnight in New Hampshire where we were vacationing.

Just a couple weeks before I wrote this paragraph, in March 2020, I spoke with a very well-known person who felt that the COVID-19 virus was manufactured in a laboratory and designed to kill off older people (to reduce the government's liability of taking care of its oldest generation).

He has a unique view on this and other opinions. If you want to read up on it, go to bernydohrmann.com. I also bought his latest book and read it. Why? Not because I believe everything he believes, but because it expands my worldview and forces me to think in new and unique ways.

What Do I Do Next?

You've identified an opportunity. Now what do you do? This is unique to every company and situation. Books are written on this very subject, but how does this relate to you? Of course, we think you should engage an expert (cough … cough … our team ☺).

One approach is to think energetically about your issue or opportunity. Here is one way to do this.

Start by thinking deeply about the opportunity, the ramifications of following it, your SWOT analysis, and most importantly, ask yourself, *What is my gut telling me*? Look for patterns. There may be intuitive patterns (unseen ones) that are just as valid as patterns in a sudoku game. Where is your intuitive energy leading you? Why is it going there? How can you ride this energetic wave? Who are the energetic players?

If you are new to the energy game, here are two ways to assist you. The first is to feel how your heart reacts when you visualize successfully implementing the opportunity. If your heart feels like it is expanding, then that's a good indicator that you should follow it.

The second technique is to use muscle testing as outlined earlier to tap into your gut feeling/intuition involving a question or dilemma. Remember, the harder it is to pull your fingers apart or for someone else to push your arm down, the more your intuition is advising you that your strength/reaction is confirming your truth.

Before You Go

It was such an honor to spend time with you throughout your reading of this book. I'd like to take just a few more minutes to make a request. It's not a large one.

If you enjoyed this book, would you be so kind as to take a moment, go to Amazon (www.amazon.com), and look up this title, and leave a short review? Even if you only had time to go through a couple of chapters, you will be able to leave a review and, if you desire, go back later and add to it once you've had a chance to complete the book. Your first impressions are very useful.

Books succeed by the kind, generous time readers take to leave honest reviews. This is how other readers learn about books that are most beneficial for them to buy. You can take part in wealth building in this manner. To this end, I thank you in advance for this very kind gesture of appreciation. It means the world to me.

Thank you so much.

Robert Slayton

Thank You to Our Reviewers

Renzo Luzzatti

US-Rx Care
877-252-0790
www.us-rxcare.com

Renzo was amazing in his feedback and is the smartest person I know when it comes to understanding the PBM space and how to cut costs.

Brad Dumke

Equity Health
844-855-8422
www.EquityHealth.net

Brad is a person fighting the good fight with me about reducing costs while improving employee's health outcomes. We can tap into his expertise to help with creating a plan that works for employers.

Kush Banerjee

Leapfrog Group
https://www.leapfroggroup.org/

Kush helped me flesh out the section where I included their safety ratings. Leapfrog Group has been collecting, analyzing, and publishing data on safety and quality in health care for 20 years.

Chris Ault (and his wife, Nurse Deb)

Ault International Medical Management, LLC
https://aim-m.com/

The finest Medical Management company I've found with amazing people running it. They help drive positive outcomes for employees. I've used them for my family's issues.

Nelson Griswold

NextGen Benefits
https://nextgenbenefits.network/
615-369-0618

The person who helped start me on this journey to becoming a sought-after Adviser. He is an amazing person, author, speaker, and columnist for several trade magazines.

CHAPTER 8: THANK YOU TO OUR REVIEWERS

Ryan Spencer

Next Gen Mastermind Partner, Co-Founder of City on a Hill Health
317-522-9966
https://cityonahillhealth.com/

Ryan is an expert in coalitions and helped outline the differences, how to avoid the "watch outs" and how to ensure the most value.

Appendix

Insurance Terminology

NETWORKS: PPO, POS, HMO, EPO, None

NOTE: These are general terms. Each insurance company applies them differently to each category.

PPO is the broadest – you can go to any doctor or hospital in the network with no referral. This also includes out of network coverage (in general, NEVER go out of network if you can avoid it)
POS – You can go to any specialist in the network WITH A REFERRAL from your primary care doctor (PCP) (or primary care women's doctor PCWP). (Note: some plans in Illinois are based on the POS, but don't enforce this referral rule).
HMO – Your PCP or PCWP will refer you only to specialists within their smaller Independent Physicians Association (IPA). The PCP will only refer to a specialist outside of their IPA if their IPA does not contain that specialist.
EPO - you can go to any doctor or hospital in the network with no referral. There is NO out of network coverage. This is not available in all states.
None – Reference-based pricing (RBP) does not typically use a network, but will pay based upon a "reference" price.

This is typically a percentage of Medicare. Office visits may be 120% to 150% of the Medicare reimbursement for a doctor and major surgery may be $150% to 170% of the Medicare reimbursement for that surgery.

NOTE: Most networks pay 250% to 600% of the Medicare reimbursement, so that's why going with a plan that uses RBP saves money.

NOTE 2: Some doctors and hospitals may not accept the payment offered, so one MUST have a good system to indemnify the employee in case there is a disagreement. Some companies will negotiate the price upfront (if possible) which eliminates problems.

What is a copay?

Copays are what you pay first before you receive service.

If your plan says "Copay, then 100%" (sometimes it also says "deductible waived"), then this means that you only pay your copay and nothing more. For example, if you go to your doctor's office and have a $30 copay. This means you'd only pay $30 to see the doctor, even if the actual cost of the visit is $200.

If your plan says "Copay, then deductible and coinsurance," then this means you'd pay your copay (e.g. $250 for surgery), then you'd pay either the bill (if less than your annual deductible) or up to your deductible, then you'd pay a percentage of the rest of the bill until you reach your out-of- pocket maximum.

What is a deductible?

A deductible is typically an amount that you pay for a bill AFTER copays have been applied and BEFORE the insurance company pays.

NOTE: If a copay says "Copay then 100%", that typically means there is no deductible for that item. This would typically be the case for Prescriptions and Office Visits.

NOTE2: In some states, there is a brand-name drug deductible. In this case, you'd pay the deductible first before the co-pay kicks in. For example, there is a $100/year drug deductible. Your first prescription costs $200. You'd pay the first $100, then your copay for that tier or drug. The rest of the year, you'd just pay the copay.

What is Coinsurance?

Coinsurance means that you pay a percentage of the next set of bills, so 80% coinsurance means that the insurance company pays 80% of the bill and you pay 20%. Most of the time coinsurance kicks in after a deductible is met but before you meet your out of pocket maximum.

Example:

First, let's set some items on your insurance policy.

Your copay for surgery is $250/surgery.

Your annual deductible is $3,000.

You pay 20% after you meet your deductible.

Your maximum coinsurance out of pocket is $2,000 (in addition to your deductible of $3,000). On a Summary of Benefits and Coverage, this would read as $5,000 Maximum Out of Pocket.

You have not met any of your deductibles/out of pocket maximums yet.

You go in for surgery (knee surgery).

The total bill is $20,000.

$3,000 Deductible $2,000 Coinsurance

Step 1, you pay your $250 surgery copay. This comes off your coinsurance: $2,000 - $250 = $1,750 left of your coinsurance out of pocket maximum. $20,000 bill - $250 = $19,750 left of the bill.

Step 2, you pay your deductible of $3,000. $19,750 left of the bill - $3,000 deductible = $16,750 left. You have met your deductible maximum for the year.

$16,750 left of the original bill

Step 3, you pay 20% of the bill until you reach your maximum coinsurance amount left ($1,750). The insurance company pays 80% of that portion of the bill.

20% of $8,750 = $1,750 (the insurance company pays $7,000 which is equal to that 80% portion). You have met your co-insurance maximum and your deductible maximum.

Step 4, the insurance company pays the rest of the bill. $16,750 - $1,750 - $7,000 = $8,000. This $8,000 is paid by the insurance company.

Health Savings Accounts (HSA)

HSAs allow you to open a bank account and put money away to pay for medical, dental, vision, chiropractic, prescription, and other medically necessary items and deduct it from your taxes. NOTE: Whatever money you put into your bank account is what you deduct off your taxes. YOU DO NOT NEED TO USE THE FUNDS. Whatever money is left at the end of the year rolls over and you can put more money away into the bank account.

In order to be able to do this you need to be on an HSA compatible health plan (it will say it is or ask your Administrator).

There are maximum contributions you can make to your HSA bank account. Please refer to the following link for more information: http://bit.ly/GvtHSAInfo

NOTE: If a husband and wife are both 55+ and both want to do a catch-up contribution. Then 2 HSA bank accounts need to be opened.

Health Reimbursement Arrangements (HRA)

This is simply an arrangement funded by the employer whereby they will pay for certain eligible medical expenses up to a pre-arranged amount. For example, the employer chooses a $6,000 deductible health plan, but only wants the employee to be responsible for $1,500 of that deductible. The HRA would be written such that once an employee reaches $1,500, then they may submit their subsequent bills to the HRA administrator to be reimbursed.

HRAs are much more flexible than HSAs in that you can designate certain items to be covered (such as a particular medication not covered by a formulary). The employer also does not pay for any claims not incurred whereas if an employer contributes to a person's HSA account, that money is transferred to the employee's personal HSA bank account without regard to claims (it's a sunk cost).

Endnotes

1. Chayefsky, Paddy. "Network." IMDB. Accessed June 27, 2021. https://www.imdb.com/title/tt0074958
2. Girod, Christopher S., Houchens, Paul R., Liner, David M., Naugle, Andrew L., Norris, Doug, and Weltz, Scott A. "2020 Milliman Medical Index." Milliman. May 21, 2020. https://www.milliman.com/en/insight/2020-Milliman-Medical-Index
3. Diabetes In Control Website. "Cost of Diabetes Non-Adherence $11,000 Yearly Per Patient." Diabetes In Control. Accessed June 27, 2021. http://www.diabetesincontrol.com/cost-of-diabetes-non-adherence-11000-yearly-per-patient
4. Freed, Steve. "The True Cost of Diabetes and Preventing It." Diabetes In Control. Accessed June 27, 2021. http://www.diabetesincontrol.com/the-true-cost-of-diabetes-and-preventing-it
5. Kim, Chul and Prasad, Vinay. "Cancer Drugs Approved on the Basis of a Surrogate End Point and Subsequent Overall Survival." JAMA Internal Medicine. Accessed June 27, 2021. https://pubmed.ncbi.nlm.nih.gov/26502403
6. Fresques, Hannah. Doctors Prescribe More of a Drug If They Receive Money From a Pharma Company Tied To

It. Propublica.org. December 20, 2019. https://www.propublica.org/article/doctors-prescribe-more-of-a-drug-if-they-receive-money-from-a-pharma-company-tied-to-it
7. Freed, Steve. "The True Cost of Diabetes and Preventing It." Diabetes In Control.
8. Ducharme, Jamie. "Misdiagnosing Cancer Is More Common Than We Think." Boston Magazine. Accessed June 25, 2021. https://www.bostonmagazine.com/health/2013/01/31/study-cancer-misdiagnose
9. Weinstein M.D., Stuart, Yelin PhD, Edward H. and Watkins-Castillo PhD, Sylvia I. "The Burden of Musculoskeletal Diseases in The United States: The Big Picture." Boneandjointburden.org. Accessed June 27, 2021. https://www.boneandjointburden.org/2014-report/i0/big-picture
10. Orenstein, Beth W. "10 Common Outpatient Procedures." Healthgrades.com. June 27, 2019. https://www.healthgrades.com/right-care/tests-and-procedures/10-common-outpatient-procedures
11. Neiman PhD, Andrea B., Ruppar PhD., Todd, Ho M.D., Michael, Garber M.D., Larry, Weidle PharmD, Paul U., Hong M.D., Yuling, George MD., Mary G. and Thorpe M.D., Phoebe G. "CDC Grand Rounds: Improving Medication Adherence for Chronic Disease Management — Innovations and Opportunities." CDC. November 17, 2017. https://www.cdc.gov/mmwr/volumes/66/wr/mm6645a2.htm
12. Van Such, Monica, Lohr M.D., Robert, Beckman M.D., Thomas and Naessens ScD, James M. "Extent of

CHAPTER 8: ENDNOTES

Diagnostic Agreement Among Medical Referrals." Wiley Online Library. April 4, 2017. https://onlinelibrary.wiley.com/doi/abs/10.1111/jep.12747
13. Kim, Chul and Prasad, Vinay. "Cancer Drugs Approved on the Basis of a Surrogate End Point and Subsequent Overall Survival."
14. Rowling, J.K. "Harry Potter and the Sorcerer's Stone." Amazon. Accessed June 27, 2021. https://www.amazon.com/Harry-Potter-Sorcerers-Stone-Rowling/dp/0590353403

ROBERT C SLAYTON, MS Ed - BIOGRAPHY

Robert has been in the industry for almost 20 years and specializes in helping employers control and reduce up to 40% a heretofore unmanageable cost while at the same time making sure employees have better health outcomes, lower deductibles, and lower premiums.

He works with employers to manage the healthcare supply chain to create superior outcomes.

He is an expert on health insurance and has been quoted in trade magazines and the popular press (such as Crains, Chicago Tribune, US News & World Report, MSNBC.com, FoxNews, The Washington Examiner, and Yahoo Hotjobs). He is co-author of the Amazon best selling book entitled: NextGeneration

Healthcare. Proven Secrets of Managing the Healthcare Value Chain to Improve Outcomes and Reduce Costs.

Every year, employers see their investment in employee healthcare increase. Most executives feel helpless and are unable to reign in those costs which now represent their number two or number three budget line item.

Historically, it was nearly impossible to predict and control a company's healthcare budget, but today, due to new solutions, strategies, technology, and a wealth of data, business leaders can (and are) taking back control of their healthcare budgets to reclaim trapped profits while actually creating healthier, happier employees that are more fulfilled and more productive.

As a next generation benefits adviser, he has the privilege of helping employers achieve those game-changing results and break through the status quo of just accepting increasing healthcare costs year after year. He works with over 40 colleagues from around the country to design and implement programs that benefit both the employer and employee.

Brokering insurance and negotiating the lowest cost increase is no longer a sustainable, viable, or preferred approach to managing a company's healthcare investment. What's required today is a legitimate consultative and strategic approach that solves the problem long-term.

This new approach is healthcare supply chain management. This model allows companies to apply the same effective cost-control practices they leverage in other parts of the organization to their healthcare costs – the process eliminates wasted expenses, redirects dollars to produce a measurable ROI, and optimizes the employee healthcare experience creating a more loyal, productive, and profitable workforce.

If you want happier and more productive employees, and a long-term healthcare strategy that adds to your EBITA, then let's chat. It is not certain that his approach will work for your organization, but Robert's willing to invest a few minutes to find out and answer your questions.

Robert is Past President of the Illinois State Association of Health Underwriters (ISAHU) and Past Legislative Co-Chair for the DuPage Association of Health Underwriters (DAHU).

He holds a Master's of Science Degree in Education in Counseling from Northern Illinois University and a Bachelor's Degree in Psychology from the University of Michigan (with a minor in International Business).

NEXTGEN BENEFITS | NETWORK   NEXTGEN BENEFITS | MASTERMIND